UNLOCK

LEVERAGING THE HIDDEN INTELLIGENCE
IN YOUR LEADERSHIP TEAM

ROB PYNE

Praise for Rob's work

'Rob's engaging and insightful style has helped my leadership team work together to create and roll out our strategy. His ideas and frameworks have helped us to collaborate, to do our best thinking, and to turn our ideas into concrete plans and real business impact.'

Steve O'Connor, CEO, JCDecaux Australia New Zealand

'Rob has helped galvanise my leadership team, tackle big issues and develop strategy through the memorable and meaningful offsites we've done together.'

Paul Sigaloff, Managing Director ANZ, Verizon Media

'Every leadership team in the country could learn something from this book. It's full of clear ideas and practical solutions to the challenges that leadership teams face.'

Stephanie Douglas-Neal, General Manager, PHD Media

'*Unlock* is packed full of ideas to bring your leadership team together – so you can set your company apart.'

Andrew Livingston, Executive Director, Mediahub Asia Pacific

'Rob's big ideas and practical tools have really helped my senior team make a positive shift in how we think, and how we work together.'

Johanna Lowe, Director of Marketing and Communications, University of Sydney

'Rob's ideas and tools don't just sound good, they work even better.'

Richard Curtis, CEO, FutureBrand Australia

'The great thing about *Unlock* is the ideas and insights presented by Rob are based on real-world examples and his deep understanding of the theories behind them. *Unlock*'s content is highly accessible and you can start applying Rob's advice immediately. Rob has made a real difference to the way we operate as a leadership team and organisation.'

Andrew Byrne, Managing Director, Oztech Intelligent Systems

'Stuffed with fascinating insight, practical suggestions and real world examples, Rob Pyne's new book *Unlock* is a guidebook for leadership teams along the path to realising their collective potential. The result is a thought-provoking look at leadership from an angle that is critically important but too often ignored.'

David Roddick, Former Chief Sales Officer, Foxtel Media and Adshel

'This book will help every leader unlock the potential in their team.'

Sarah Gallon, General Manager of Brand, Creative and Media, Tourism Australia

Acknowledgements

One day in June 2020, my mentor Dr Amy Silver told me it was my time to write a book. I'd been considering it for a while. The middle of a pandemic, with work on hold, seemed like a good opportunity. I started writing it that week.

Kath Walters coached me through the structure and taught me how writers write.

Col Fink showed me how to build a book point by point and section by section – to take a mass of ideas and convert them into a format that can read cover to cover or be dipped in and out of.

The following people gave me useful feedback on the first draft: Alissa Barrett, Andrew Byrne, Stephanie Douglas-Neal, Max Eburne, Andy Gaunt, Mark Mansour, David Roddick and Dr Amy Silver.

To all the leaders and teams I've worked with, it has been a privilege to help you, and to learn from you.

Thanks to the team at Publish Central for turning a manuscript into a real book.

To my children, Emma, Lucy and Kate, for keeping it real and making everything worthwhile.

And to my wonderful wife, Monica – for your strength and support.

*Dedicated to the bright memories of Roger Pyne,
and the bright futures of Emma, Lucy and Kate Pyne.*

Disclaimer

The material in this publication is of the nature of general comment only, and does not represent professional advice. It is not intended to provide specific guidance for particular circumstances and it should not be relied on as the basis for any decision to take action or not take action on any matter which it covers. Readers should obtain professional advice where appropriate, before making any such decision. To the maximum extent permitted by law, the author and publisher disclaim all responsibility and liability to any person, arising directly or indirectly from any person taking or not taking action based on the information in this publication.

Contents

Introduction

BACK IN 1984 …

When I was ten, I loved the role-playing game Dungeons and Dragons.

Once a month, six of us would gather for a whole day, with the Dungeon Master challenging us to find treasure, fight evil, earn 'experience points' and master our crafts as Wizard, Fighter or Thief.

It was always the highlight of my month. Why? The Dungeon Master set a difficult and significant challenge. We had to work together and think creatively to solve it. We each had clear roles and skills we brought to the group. And the leader facilitated the group effectively. The whole experience was, in a word, inspiring.

FAST-FORWARD TO 2021 …

I recently had a conversation with David, an ex-colleague. We talked about what makes a good leadership team, and what productive leadership team meetings feel like. I said leaders should show up for these meetings feeling positive and prepared. And they should leave the sessions feeling inspired.

David said, 'I've never been in a leadership team like that. And I've never even heard of one.' It's true that, according to research from McKinsey in 'Teamwork at the Top', just 20 per cent of executives rate their leadership team as 'high performing'. So, David's experience might be typical.

And yet, almost every company's strategy, its very survival, is predicated on having an effective leadership team. We assume our leadership team will be high performing, but 80 per cent of the time it's not.

I've been lucky enough to work in, and with, a wide range of leadership teams, and I've seen a number of them become inspiring.

In this book, I explore what holds leadership teams back. And I explore ways to make them better – more effective, more productive and more strategic. And maybe even make them as inspiring as a day spent playing Dungeons and Dragons to a ten-year-old.

THE EVOLUTION OF YOUR LEADERSHIP TEAM

Perhaps you lead an executive leadership team or a functional leadership team. Or perhaps you're a member of one these leadership teams. Whatever your role, you're probably reading this book because you want your leadership team to evolve beyond where it is today.

You may be aware of Bruce Tuckman's four-step model from 'Developmental sequence in small groups' that describes how teams develop: *Forming, Storming, Norming and Performing.* Maybe you're also aware this model is from way back in 1965. And it seems to imply that if you sit back and let nature take its course, your team will one day simply find itself 'performing'. That's not my experience of modern leadership teams.

....
**Leadership teams tend towards mediocrity or mayhem –
if you don't pay close attention to facilitating team growth.**
....

This book provides a 21st-century take on leadership teams, piecing together a wide range of academic work and real-world case studies to help you build a better leadership team.

DISCOVERING THE COLLECTIVE INTELLIGENCE OF YOUR LEADERSHIP TEAM

This book is organised around the three types of intelligence every leadership team needs:

- emotional intelligence – to navigate challenges thrown up by people and culture
- creative-analytical intelligence – to provide the critical thinking required for complex strategic challenges
- practical intelligence – to deliver on strategy and turn all the talk into action.

Each of these three types of intelligence has three crucial elements – making up what I call the nine building blocks of team intelligence. (I explain these nine building blocks further in chapter 2.)

Importantly, these three types of intelligence, and the building blocks that support them, are not just the properties of the leadership team's *individual members*.

....

The three types of intelligence, and their building blocks, are forms of *collective intelligence*, where the whole leadership team can be more intelligent than the sum of its parts.

....

Throughout this book, I lay out the evidence for this collective intelligence, focusing on the following:

- Teams have their own level of emotional intelligence that can be higher than the individual members' emotional intelligence – if you lay the right foundations.
- A team's ability to solve problems is an emergent property, based on the team dynamics, not just the team members' individual abilities.
- Teams often struggle with delivering their plans and projects – but your team can create a huge productivity gain by applying your collective practical intelligence.

I use this research-based approach to help you create an environment where your team becomes collectively intelligent. This is what I mean when I refer to teams that are smarter than the sum of their parts.

NAVIGATING THIS BOOK

If you like to read from the start to the finish, this book is organised in a logical progression through the three layers of intelligence for leadership teams:

- Part I focuses on why leadership teams are different from other teams – and why leading them requires new skills. It also introduces the three types of intelligence and the nine building blocks in more detail. The differences between leadership teams and other types of teams are important and, in my view, underappreciated. These differences mean leadership teams require a conscious change of approach from the leader and the leadership team.
- Part II looks at emotional intelligence, with chapters 3 to 5 delving into the building blocks within this type of intelligence – laying foundations, building behavioural norms, and checking in.
- Part III focuses on creative-analytical intelligence, with chapters 6 to 8 covering thinking deeper, thinking wider and thinking further ahead.
- Part IV turns to practical intelligence, and chapters 9 to 11 outline the importance of making plans, tracking progress and scheduling pit stops.
- Part V pulls all of the ideas in this book together, outlining the journey your leadership team needs to take and the leader's role in this journey. I estimate it takes around 12 months to unlock the potential of a leadership team, and so in the final chapter I outline what those 12 months might look like, taking the themes and ideas in the book and laying out a transformation plan for the team itself, along with suggestions on how to track progress.

Of course, reading a book from cover to cover is not always realistic for many leaders. So, this book is also designed for readers to dip into. Each chapter is self-contained, so you can head to the part or chapter that feels most relevant to your leadership team right now.

Where are you now, and where are you headed?

Typically, I'm called in to provide leadership support in one of three situations. Chances are, you and your team are in one of these situations right now.

Building a new leadership team

Perhaps you're starting a new leadership team. Or you have arrived in a new job and want to reset the leadership team. Maybe the leadership team has gone through several personnel changes, so a reset is possible.

If this is you, you may want to start with the chapters in part II on emotional intelligence, because you'll need to lay the foundations of the team.

Fixing a current leadership team

As the leader, perhaps you're spending too much of your time and energy fixing problems between the team members. Communication is poor. Projects and tasks that have been committed to don't get done, because people are 'too busy'. Overall, your leadership team is under-performing to some degree, and you want to iron out these issues.

If this is you, you may want to start by having your team take my Team Intelligence Diagnostic (available at robpyne.online/unlock) and then read the chapters of this book that address your team's lowest scores. For example, if the diagnostic identifies your key issues are in delivery, you can go straight to part IV on practical intelligence.

Developing a strategic plan

Perhaps you need to develop a strategic plan for your whole functional team or organisation. Some serious thinking is required. But you don't want the same old 'Groundhog Day' of endless discussions resulting in a blue-sky strategy, which then gets forgotten.

If this is you, you may want to take a quick look at the chapters in part II, to ensure you have strong, emotionally intelligent foundations. Then head to part III to look at unlocking the creative-analytical intelligence of your team. Finish with part IV, looking at how to translate your strategy into robust plans and track progress.

A note on the stories

This book features many stories based on my experiences running more than 500 leadership team offsites, strategy planning sessions, team-building event workshops, conferences and training days. To protect client confidentiality, I have changed the names of participants and companies, and changed other identifiable details. The key learnings and observations remain intact.

Accessing online resources

To help you get the most out of the book, I've also created a suite of online resources, assessments and tools (available at robpyne. online/unlock). These are referenced in the relevant sections of the book.

Taking action

The book is designed to be easy to read and for the information provided to be easy to turn into action. In particular:

- The detailed table of contents allows you to quickly find the relevant ideas to help you.
- Each chapter ends with a clear summary, suggested actions and next steps.
- Chapter 13 provides a roadmap to take your leadership team on a 365-day journey of growth.
- The appendix outlines a checklist of areas to focus on, broken down by each chapter.

So let's get started – beginning with the special characteristics of leadership teams, and the specific challenges they face.

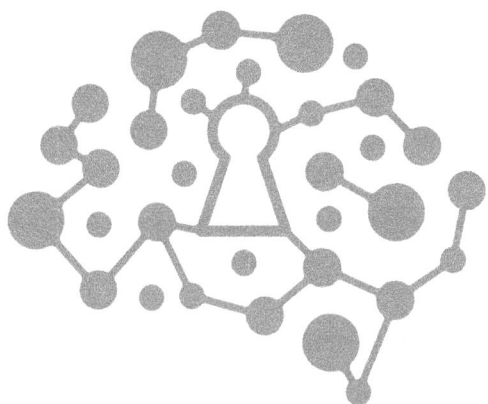

PART I

THE POTENTIAL OF
LEADERSHIP TEAMS

THE SPARSE INTERSECTION OF LEADERSHIP AND TEAMS

If you want to understand more about *leadership*, a quick search of the books available on the topic on Amazon.com means you'll be spoilt for choice – with more than 60,000 titles to choose from.

If you want to understand more about *teams*, a search will again reveal more than 60,000 books you could buy from Amazon.

However, a search for books on 'leadership teams' reveals just 16 matches, of which only four are focused specifically on this topic.

(With the publication of this book, you can make that five.)

We need to close this gap in Amazon's bookshelves, and in leaders' access to resources, for two reasons.

First, leadership is no longer something you can do alone as a 'one-man band'.

....
Leadership is more a collective pursuit than a solo performance.
....

Almost all of the books on leadership I've read focus entirely on the leader's individual journey.

Second, if you explored the 60,000+ books on teams, very few of them are written specifically for *leadership* teams. And yet my experience from being in three corporate leadership teams and coaching many others shows that leadership teams are very different – for reasons I explore in chapter 1.

YOU CAN UNLOCK THE COLLECTIVE INTELLIGENCE OF YOUR TEAM

Tucked away in Cambridge, Massachusetts, is the MIT Centre for Collective Intelligence. As I cover in chapter 2, they, and other researchers, have found that teams can have a mind of their own, where they are better at solving problems together than would be predicted from the team members' individual intelligence.

They call a team's collective intelligence the *C Factor*, and this idea underpins this book because it lends scientific evidence to an idea we know in our hearts: that teams can be more than the sum of their parts.

Using their research and applying it to leadership teams introduces some intriguing possibilities. In the following chapters, I explore their research in depth to find out:

- Under what conditions does a team become smarter than the sum of its parts?
- What gender split makes for the most intelligent teams?
- What social and emotional skills underpin team intelligence?

The available research tells us a great deal about running our leadership teams, building the emotional connections between members, and having effective problem-solving discussions. But it leaves a gap – once a team has come up with an intelligent solution, how well do they execute their plans?

We need to create leadership teams with an unrelenting focus on alignment, accountability and action. This book is all about showing you how.

....

We already know in our heart that teams can be more than the sum of their parts.

....

1

Differences.
Why leadership teams are different – and how they can flourish.

Two hours into a leadership offsite with a fast-growing alcohol brand, I asked, 'Can you tell me how often you meet and what you talk about in your leadership team meetings?'

They described their weekly meetings, and how in those meetings they went through the current workload in each part of the business.

I asked if they ever looked at whole-of-business performance, such as the profit and loss, and I asked if they ever had other types of meetings that were more focused on the longer term.

They didn't.

I ventured a suggestion: 'So you're probably more like a management team then?'

It was a lightbulb moment for this team. They realised they'd been focused on managing the workload and people in their areas, but they weren't leading. They weren't collectively setting a direction. They weren't thinking holistically about the whole business. The only person who was thinking more broadly was the entrepreneurial founder and CEO, Amelia.

Amelia decided she needed to build a proper leadership team. The first step in doing this is to carefully define what a leadership team is and what it does – and how it's different from the current team set-up.

Leadership teams are different from management teams.

....
Leadership teams take a whole-of-business perspective to set the direction, build the culture and drive performance.
....

Management teams, on the other hand, are focused on managing people and tasks to deliver on the leadership's strategy.

Leadership teams are also qualitatively different from the other teams we participate in and lead in our careers. A failure to understand the differences will limit your team's impact – and limit your collective ability.

LEADERSHIP TEAMS ARE UNLIKE OTHER TEAMS

Reflect on the teams you've worked in across your career.

Likely you started out working in what we can call a *functional team* (FT), where you were a doer – sometimes called 'an individual contributor' these days – and your team had a relatively narrow focus on delivering products and services.

Over time, you got promoted to more influential roles within functional teams. You made a more significant contribution and became a manager.

Eventually, you might have joined a *functional leadership team* (FLT), where you became responsible for integrating work across the various parts of your function and setting the direction of your area to contribute to the organisation's overall strategy.

If you then became the functional leader, you probably moved onto the *executive leadership team* (ELT), where you got to help create the organisation's overall strategy.

And if you went one step further and became the leader of the organisation, you became responsible for leading the top team.

This book is written for the members and leaders of FLTs and ELTs, which I combine and call leadership teams (LTs).

As you think about your experience, can you see the differences between the functional teams and leadership teams? How did you find the transition into your first leadership team role?

In my experience and observation, people often take time to adapt to the different behaviours and expectations of leadership teams. They've taken a big step up, but are rarely given any tips, guidance or training into how to be effective in a leadership team.

Leadership training – if you get it – tends to focus on how you lead your functional team, your direct reports, and neglects your role as a member of a leadership team.

Rohan's two hats

Rohan was the Head of IT at Excore Services. He had a moment of vulnerability with his team, and owned up to feeling unable to contribute much to discussions beyond his functional expertise. Each leadership team meeting included a section to discuss IT, for example, and Rohan would provide an update. Then he would be utterly silent on almost every other topic – from finance to sales, from HR to marketing.

The group agreed that in a leadership team, it's not just your right to comment on issues outside your functional area – it's your responsibility.

They called this the 'two hats rule'. In the leadership team, Rohan needed to sometimes wear his functional hat as the Head of IT. But he also needed to take that hat off and put on a second hat, the Organisational Hat, so he could contribute to whole-of-business discussions.

That didn't go all the way to solving Rohan's issue. With a bit of one-on-one coaching, he decided he could implement two further strategies to feel more comfortable contributing. First, he could spend some time getting to know the other areas of the business. Second, he could concentrate on asking pertinent questions, not on trying to have all the answers.

Rohan had learnt that leadership teams are different – and a step-up – from functional teams.

The four ways leadership teams are different

Comparing leadership teams to functional teams highlights four differences. Each one helps leaders think about how they get the best out of their leadership team, and how they must adapt their leadership style to their 'top team'.

These four differences relate to the leadership team's:

- Purpose: *Why* the team exists
- People: *Who* is in the team
- Product: *What* the team produces; its output
- Processes: *How* the team operates

Table 1.1 outlines these four areas, and how they are different between functional and leadership teams. The following sections then explore these areas in more detail.

Purpose: *Why* the team exists

In *Senior Leadership Teams: What it Takes to Make Them Great*, authors Ruth Wageman, Debra Nunes, James Burruss and Richard Hackman outline that a 'compelling direction' is a pre-requisite for leadership teams:

> In the best leadership teams we have studied, we discovered that their leaders found a way to provide a crystal-clear sense of the team's unique added value in advancing the organisation's strategy.

So the first time I work with a leadership team, I often ask them, 'What value does this leadership team create that wouldn't be created if you didn't meet up?'

The answer to this question should not be nebulous. To break the question down and arrive at the team's real value, I ask them to complete the following:

- First of all, write down all the stakeholders who have an interest in what this leadership team does.
- Then for each stakeholder group, write down what value you create for them.
- Then prioritise these and agree on the most important types of value the team creates, as well as a list of their stakeholders.

Table 1.1: The four areas of difference between functional and leadership teams

	Functional teams	Leadership teams
WHY **The purpose of the team**	Co-ordinate and deliver the work in one area to deliver results Focus on activities in the short term Follow the existing behavioural standards and cultural rules	Integrate the work of many functions to deliver results Focus on the medium- and long-term vision and strategy Define and role-model the behavioural standards and culture rules
WHO **The people in the team**	Doers Co-located Similar backgrounds Inclusive Highly interdependent	Functional leaders Not co-located Different backgrounds Representative More independent
WHAT **The product of the team**	Lists of actions: what do we need to do?	Decisions and strategies that shape direction: where do we need to go?
HOW **The processes of the team**	Practical thinking, problem-solving, planning	Whole-of-business integrated, strategic thinking

This process allows the leadership team to quickly move into answering the *How* and *What* questions: *'If that's the value we need to create, how should we meet and what should we talk about?'*

People: *Who* is in the team

Many leadership teams are made up of the heads of each functional group. If this is the make-up of your leadership team, chances are your basic concept of the leadership team is that it shares information and integrates functions. And, therefore, you need one person representing each function.

However, leadership teams can also include senior individual contributors who don't themselves oversee a large team – for example, the legal counsel or corporate strategy lead.

If you are building (or refreshing) your leadership team, you may want to consider slightly broader criteria for the make-up of the team than simply grouping functional heads. Also consider the following:

- *Size:* An ideal leadership team has around five to nine people in it. (See, for example, Jacques Neatby's rundown in 'The ballooning executive team'.) This size allows everyone to contribute different perspectives but is still small enough to make decisions. A team larger than nine can easily become too unwieldy to make decisions and have debates, and can instead tend towards low-value updates on each member's functional area.
- *Representation:* To integrate the work of the various parts of the organisation, you do need to have representation from all major business units, and a plan for two-way communication if you leave any departments out.
- *Cognitive diversity:* To solve problems effectively, you will benefit from having different styles of thinking (for more on this, see chapter 3).

These three areas can represent challenges for the leader of an existing team, as well as opportunities for the creator of a new team.

Don't become too big to make decisions

When the leadership team becomes too big to make decisions, several consequences ensue. Some people are reticent and become disengaged, particularly those from the smaller functions. Meetings take a long time as multiple perspectives are canvassed. An informal 'real' leadership team often then develops – likely two or three people who make the real decisions and leave the official leadership team as a stripped-down information-sharing forum.

Don't be representative all the time

Having a single person representing each function encourages siloed thinking – where people give an opinion based on their function. This has value but makes negotiating whole-of-business solutions harder. You need the 'two hats rule' (see the 'Rohan's two hats' case study, earlier in this chapter).

You may also find each leadership team member considers their primary team to be their functional team, and their secondary team to be the leadership team. This is a natural tendency, because they spend much more time with their functional team; however, it can promote tension between 'the team you're in' versus 'the team you lead'.

One leader I worked with was explicit about correcting this, saying to his direct reports, 'This leadership team has to be your A-Team'.

Understand diversity is not smooth

In leadership teams, you will get better outcomes if you have a cognitively diverse team. People who think differently bring different experiences, expertise and thinking styles to a problem.

Often you get a certain amount of cognitive diversity simply by having different functional representatives. Perhaps the heads of Sales, Finance and Operations, and Legal all speak different languages (metaphorically at least) and have different backgrounds and problem-solving styles.

This level of cognitive diversity becomes more likely as you move from a functional team into a leadership team. Previously, perhaps your functional team contained only finance people with similar backgrounds and knowledge. Now, being in a leadership team requires working much more closely with Sales, Operations, IT and HR, and learning the different ways they see business issues.

Dealing with this increased variety of languages and thinking styles is mentally tiring. It's much easier to work with people who see the world the same way you do – because you're working from the same assumptions and shared perspective. But to get the most from cognitive diversity, you need to listen more, understand more deeply, and challenge your own beliefs.

If not managed well, cognitive diversity can be a negative: each leadership team member may find the discussion, dialogue and debate frustrating and unproductive.

Create opportunities for connection
The challenges connected to each of these features – size, representation and diversity – are more prevalent and more consequential for leadership teams. This is due to the one other way a leadership team differs from a functional team: frequency of interaction.

If your organisation has offices, it's likely the leadership team sit with their functional colleagues. The majority of their daily interactions will be within their function. That means some members of the leadership team can go weeks between seeing or talking to each other. Of course, natural pairings such as the Heads of Sales and Marketing might collaborate daily. But other pairings may rarely have contact between leadership team meetings. Building emotional connections between the team is more difficult.

....

Functional teams develop an emotional connection from their day-to-day conversations. Leadership teams need to think more carefully to build a real team, with genuine interdependencies and emotional connections.

....

Product: *What* the team produces
Functional teams typically produce lists of actions and owners – who's doing what by when? They often focus on products, services, customers. And their line of sight is 'this week'. They are 'keeping the trains running', conducting business-as-usual and – hopefully – hitting targets.

Leadership teams also need these practical, action-oriented skills, of course. They need to integrate all the work across the organisation and solve significant short-term issues. But more than that, they need to generate ideas, decisions and strategies that transform the organisation and keep it ahead of the competition.

The leadership team should produce a vision of the organisation's future state, and a strategy, plan and goals to get there.

Process: *How* the team operates

Leadership team meetings also need to be set up differently compared to functional teams. These meetings often see a tension, competition even, between short-term operational issues and the long-term vision and planning. The time spent on short-term issues usually over-runs and eats up the time meant to be spent on the longer-term direction. One practical solution for leaders is to separate the different types of conversation.

In my experience, many leadership teams have just one type of meeting – say, a fortnightly or monthly catch up. These get dominated by operational issues. And they can go off on lots of low-value tangents.

Instead, you may want to hold two or more different meetings, one being operational (frequent) and one being strategic (a little less frequent). This helps to time-box the operational issues, and ensure the strategy receives regular time and attention. (For more on setting clear boundaries within leadership teams, see chapter 3.)

Martin's cabinet responsibility

Martin was the CFO of Excore Services and an experienced executive, having been on the leadership teams of several large corporations.

His contribution to a recent offsite was the notion of 'cabinet responsibility', connecting the idea with the cabinet in the Federal Government. This cabinet is made up of members who represent different functions and different groups of stakeholders. When they come together as a cabinet, they are expected to have robust debates. But when they leave the room, they must commit to the group's decision, whether they agree with it or not. They must be of one mind.

If leadership team members can't have a robust debate, they are often less committed to the final decisions. And you have a real problem if they leave the leadership team meeting and undermine the collective decisions when they report back to their functional team.

Martin's 'cabinet responsibility' rule, along with Rohan's 'two hats rule', were embraced by the entire Excore Services leadership team, and provided the behavioural foundations for a trusting and effective team. Both of these rules are specific to leadership teams, and are not often needed in lower level functional teams.

WHEN LEADERSHIP TEAMS GO BAD

'Ever since you joined, it's been all about you – it's been like "The Sean Show" around here.'

These words set off an ugly chain of events that ended in two leadership team members never speaking to each other again.

And, as the hired facilitator for Capital Partners' leadership retreat in the Southern Highlands south of Sydney, this led to one of the toughest leadership team offsites I've ever worked on.

We had been through an exercise on team effectiveness. Day one was drawing to a close, with the promise of a steak and a glass of red wine over a team dinner. I had begun to relax and wind down. I could feel the weight of managing the group's energy fade away.

I looked from face to face and asked the team, 'Is there anything else you want to mention?'

Little did I expect Georgie's grenade.

Georgie was Head of Marketing. Sean was the new chief operating officer, four months into the role.

The verbal grenade landed with a thud. Pause in the room. Then it exploded.

Sean, trying to stay calm: 'What do you mean?'

Georgie, digging the hole a little deeper: 'It's not just me saying this you know ...'

These verbal jabs went back and forth for a couple of minutes before the CEO and I attempted to diffuse the situation. The meeting broke up. People went to their rooms. The CEO called Georgie. I called Sean.

Georgie didn't come back for day two of the retreat. And because she had recently handed in her notice, she and the CEO agreed perhaps it was best if she managed her remaining tasks by working remotely for the rest of her notice period.

To my knowledge, Sean and Georgie never spoke again.

Georgie's grenade-throwing illustrates the ugly consequences of a dysfunctional leadership team.

Personal conflict within the team significantly reduces its leadership capabilities. In his 2015 TEDx Talk, conflict and collaboration expert Jim Tamm estimates that when members of a group become defensive, their ability to solve problems drops. Each member effectively loses 20 IQ points.

....

Leadership teams should be throwing ideas around, not throwing grenades at each other.

....

In Georgie and Sean's team, the focus had turned to relationship conflict, and 'fight or flight' responses had kicked in. The CEO had to turn his attention to internal mediation between warring parties, instead of focusing on the external battles the organisation needed to win. The leadership team should be co-creating the future direction, not locked into dealing with the past and present.

LEADERSHIP TEAMS ARE MORE IMPORTANT THAN EVER BEFORE

After the Southern Highlands offsite with Sean and Georgie, I did more work with Capital Partners and saw them work hard to build a trusting team. They supported each other to achieve common goals, and collectively created a high-performance culture. Three years later, they completed the successful sale of the business for $300 million.

We know that the quality of the leadership team is a significant factor when investors decide whether to buy into a company. In a McKinsey survey, outlined in 'High-performing teams: A timeless leadership topic', 90 per cent of investors believe the quality of the management team is the most important non-financial factor when evaluating an initial public offering (IPO). And they estimate an above-median financial performance is 1.9 times more likely when the top team is working together toward a shared vision.

An idea whose time has come

The term 'one-man band' is a good descriptor for prevailing concepts of leadership. This captures not only the heavy skew to men (an ABC News article from 2017 highlighted that Australia's top 200 companies included more CEOs named John than the total number of female CEOs) but also the continuing stereotype of the CEO as 'hero', the person 'calling all the shots' (military analogies abound in leadership too), inspiring the team and setting the direction.

Although most companies retain a CEO as frontman or frontwoman, these days they are rarely a one-man band. Business is too complex for one person to make all the decisions alone, so behind every good leader is a leadership team. The chief financial officer on bass, perhaps, keeping the rhythm. The chief revenue officer on lead guitar, punching out occasional solos. And the chief people officer on drums, keeping the beat going.

As the pace of change has accelerated, and the complexity of business models has increased, it is no longer feasible for one human to understand the whole business model and keep track of all the latest data across the business. You need your leadership team to help you in three ways.

- They need to help you make sense of incoming data. If you consider your business to be a complex system of interconnected parts, then having leadership team members able to report on each of the moving parts helps create collective understanding of the business's performance, and its trends.
- You need them to help you generate possible strategies and solutions – to chart a course forward. That's not to say that all decisions and strategies benefit from getting a committee involved, but it is to say that a leadership team can help you generate a wider range of options than you can do alone.

- You need them to help you turn decisions and strategies into action by leading the execution of projects and plans with their functional teams.

In this way, your leadership team helps you make better music.

....
Your leadership team help you write the song, play the music and inspire the crowd.
....

The evidence backing these ideas is clear – according to Ernst & Young's 2013 survey 'The power of many', 90 per cent of companies agree that their organisations' problems are so complex that they need teams to tackle them. As a result, the model of the solo leader making all the calls has been supplemented with a competing model of collective leadership – a group of people to help steer.

Leadership teams, boards and executive committees predominate at the top. And the amount of time spent collaborating in teams across organisations has increased by around 50 per cent in 20 years according to the Harvard Business Review article 'Collaborative overload'.

Leadership teams can lead to better overall leadership of an organisation. Not only that but, according to McKinsey's 'High-performing teams: A timeless leadership topic', being in an effective leadership team can also make individual executives five times more effective.

WHAT GOOD LEADERSHIP TEAMS DO DIFFERENTLY

In my experience of working with scores of leadership teams, around 10 per cent have serious dysfunctions, as in the Georgie and Sean situation.

Another 60 to 70 per cent are performing 'okay'. They achieve a few of their goals. Their meetings are a little painful on occasion, but they manage to avoid big blow ups. The team members get on and can even enjoy each other's company socially a few times a year. This is the reality for most leadership teams. And if we're honest with each other, it's a bit mediocre, isn't it?

The top 20 to 30 per cent of teams are performing well. They've built trust and support each other. They've set a direction for the organisation, and they communicate it often. They deliver on most of their significant goals.

Some of the leadership teams I work with are in this top 20 to 30 per cent. At the end of 2020, I worked with a seven-member leadership team from the pharmaceutical sector to conduct a review of the year and develop ideas to improve their leadership team. Using my Team Intelligence Diagnostic, a tool I have developed to determine the combined intelligence of teams I work with, I worked out they had a team IQ of 119 – that is, 19 per cent above average. This, in turn, has helped improve business performance, including growing revenue and market share in a pandemic year. (For more on the Team Intelligence Diagnostic, head to robpyne. online/unlock.)

Here are some of the areas I've seen this team perform well in, and which have contributed to their above average business performance:

- *Increased frequency of contact:* During the worst of the COVID-19 pandemic in 2020, they met every day for operational discussions for the first two months and then moved this to twice a week.
- *Improved strategy and communication:* The team had been together for several years and consistently improved how they defined and rolled out their strategy. In particular, they had a robust consultation and communication plan, making sure every employee knew how they fitted into the strategy and what was expected of them.
- *Increased connection – 'This is my team':* As a result of the increased frequency of contact during COVID-19, connections within the leadership team improved further. Team member Janice said, 'I finally realised that this is my team; I'm not just reporting here on behalf of my function'.
- *Continued leadership development:* Each leader had been given diagnostic tools to assess their skills as a leader and provide focus areas to work on.

- *Increased investment in physical connections:* They invested significant time and effort in getting the team together face to face (the team spans multiple cities in three countries) and creating shared experiences. This was important not only for strategy development, but also for learning together and building emotional connections.
- *Continued focus on tracking projects:* This team translated its strategy into a series of key initiatives, with owners, and these initiatives were regularly tracked to maintain progress.

These improvements didn't simply happen – the leader of this pharmaceutical team has made considerable effort, over several years, to develop his leadership team.

Once you have the right people in the team, lots of work remains for the leader to do if he or she wants to reap the benefits of an effective leadership team. As we'll see throughout this book, the benefits can be significant, and the costs of trying to lead without a leadership team can be high.

YOUR LEADERSHIP TEAM CAN BE MORE THAN THE SUM OF ITS PARTS

Seeing your leadership team working intelligently and collectively can inspire, instead of causing despair. It can be highly creative, instead of moderately destructive. It can be taking action, instead of making excuses.

....
The output of an effective leadership team can be described in three words: intelligent collective action.
....

Intelligent because you have captured all the intelligence and wisdom in the group to help think through problems, design solutions, and define strategies.

Collective because a real team is united behind decisions, ideas and strategies, ensuring they flow through the organisation.

Action because the leadership team's collective intelligence needs to be turned into executional excellence. Strategy is nothing without execution.

Create the environment where the team can flourish

In the main body of this book, chapters 3 to 11, I explore topics that anyone in a leadership team can act on, whether they are *the* leader of the team or *a* leader in the team.

And yet, if you want to create the right environment for the team to be more than the sum of its parts, and it you want to drive intelligent collective action, the opportunity – responsibility, even – exists for the CEO or the leader of the leadership team to set the agenda and start the conversation. This starts with asking the right questions:

- What is our strategy?
- What are our key priorities?
- How can we work as a team?
- What behaviours should we reward?
- How will we turn our ideas into action?
- How can we harness the experience and expertise of each team member?

If you lead with openness and curiosity, you can answer these questions. You can create the right environment for your team to be more than the sum of its parts, and you can create more impact as a leadership team than you could ever do as a solo leader.

What if we can't meet face to face?

At the time of writing, the world is in the middle of a pandemic. In many countries and many organisations, teams cannot meet face to face. How does this affect leadership teams?

As a facilitator, I was able to work with leadership teams in many different combinations through 2020 and 2021 – ranging from 100 per cent remote (with everyone on video) to 100 per cent face to face and socially distanced.

My experience is that with careful facilitation and attention to the technology, it is entirely possible to create the right environment for the leadership team to succeed.

That said, you do need to watch out for:

- online sessions that go too long and sap energy

- people speaking too quietly or with their back to the camera when in the same room and sharing room microphones
- scheduling not taking into account people in different time zones.

With a little planning and thought, these obstacles are easy to overcome. Remote and hybrid leadership team meetings are here to stay, and the pandemic has fast-tracked our ability to deal with the technological and social challenges.

On the bright side, this means your team members based in different states or countries can be an integral part of the leadership team's collective intelligence without having to get on an aeroplane.

Chapter summary

Leadership teams operate somewhere on a scale between toxic and terrific. They can be incredibly dysfunctional at one extreme, and inspiringly successful and impactful at the other.

Very little attention has been paid to leadership teams, with the assumption that they are just like other teams. Instead, they are fundamentally different in four ways: their purpose, their people, their product or output, and their processes.

Collective leadership is becoming even more important as our organisations navigate increasingly complex situations at ever faster speeds. Leaders need a team around them to help them make sense, make decisions and make progress.

Developing a great leadership team requires understanding these differences and complex situations, and setting up the team so that it can flourish and become smarter than the sum of its parts.

Take action

If you are *forming* a new leadership team, work with them to create a leadership team blueprint answering the why, who, what and how? Chapter 3 on the foundations of an emotionally intelligent team provides more in this area.

If you are *refreshing* your leadership team, seek to understand your team's answers on the why, who, what and how questions, and use them to update your operational approach to the leadership team, particularly how you meet and what you discuss. For more, work through chapter 3 on the foundations of an emotionally intelligent team.

If you are about to start a significant project such as a *strategy planning process*, plan the environment you create for the team to do its best thinking, and define some ground rules with the team before work begins. For more, take a look at chapter 4 on behavioural norms.

Next
In chapter 2, I outline the three challenges leadership teams face as they try to create intelligent collective action – and my model for meeting these challenges.

2

Challenges.

The three challenges for leadership teams – and the types of intelligence required.

LEADERSHIP TEAMS AREN'T EASY

The expectations on leadership teams are both extraordinarily high and usually unspoken. Much is assumed:

- *Assumption #1: Each member brings their best self.* We assume each member of the leadership team will contribute their best thinking and give their utmost energy to turn the team's plans into real impact.

- *Assumption #2: Together, the team will combine to lead the organisation.* If it's a leadership team – not a management team, or an executive committee – we assume they will combine well to deliver the functions you expect from a leader: set the direction, build the culture and drive performance.

Is 'leadership team' an oxymoron?

Hidden in these assumptions is a requirement for the team members to walk a mental tightrope. On one side, they must prove themselves, add value, be seen to be smart and make a meaningful contribution. This is the requirement of an *individual leader*.

On the other side, they must be a *team player* – that is, be supportive, make sacrifices for the team's greater good and toe the line.

In this way, the phrase 'leadership team' could be an oxymoron.

....

**We take a group of leaders. Put them into a room.
And ask them to act as followers.**

....

It is tough to be a leader and team player simultaneously.

The challenges of building a leadership team

Priyanka was the CEO and founder of a non-profit that helped Indigenous communities. Priyanka had built the non-profit into a significant presence in Queensland and Western Australia, with 50 employees. It was time to create a leadership team from the heads of Fundraising, Finance and People.

Priyanka hoped the leadership team would take some of the pressure off her, and create a potential succession plan for when she chose to hand over the reins.

That plan seems to make sense – but view it from the perspective of the three other functional heads. Priyanka was the founder and owned the relationships with government and major donors. She also formed and maintained the relationship with the board of directors. And she retained the authority to make all the critical decisions. The heads of each function were also not fully across the other functions of the business. They were unsure what the leadership team would even do, given the vast difference in status between the CEO and the three of them.

This team did not have a clear reason for being. It did not bring out the best in the individuals. And it did not have a defined way of operating.

No why. No who. No how.

Despite Priyanka's skills as a leader, and her good intentions, this group ended up less *than the sum of its parts. It chewed up significant time and mental energy, while the group's decisions were the same as if Priyanka had made them alone.*

The group failed to walk the tightrope of individual leadership and collective intelligence.

As Priyanka found, the lived experience of being in a leadership team is not so easy.

THE THREE CHALLENGES FOR LEADERSHIP TEAMS

The following sections outline the most common challenges I've seen hold back leadership teams.

Issues of people and culture

Functional heads come into the leadership team and keep their functional hat on. They fight for and defend their particular area. Instead, the leadership team members should take their functional hat off when they get to the table and put their company hat on the 'two hats rule' as discussed in chapter 1.

When a functional lead joins the leadership team for the first time, they have come from an area where they worked mainly with people in the same function. For example, the marketing director works primarily with marketing people, and they tend to think in similar ways and have a similar background. But when they join the leadership team, suddenly everyone has a different background and thinks in different ways.

....
Members of the leadership team can end up actively disliking each other, due only to their dissimilarity.
....

Also, from my experience, I see:

- leadership team members nodding along and agreeing in the meeting, but then bad-mouthing the decisions back in their functional teams

- CEOs dominating the conversation, or a small number of people doing all the talking, and the others feeling disenfranchised
- leadership teams allocating zero time to their professional development as individuals or as a team
- problem behaviours emerging within the leadership team and being left unaddressed, as the team veers towards dysfunction and distrust.

Issues of strategy

According to an MIT Sloan School survey of 4000 managers, only 28 per cent of managers can name three of their company's top priorities.

Some companies don't have a strategy to name. Or they have a strategy no-one can remember. At one company where I was working with the senior management team, I asked them to describe their strategy and one executive said, 'Was it that mountain thing the CEO presented?' and another said, 'No, there's a strategy in the team folder on the shared drive' and a third chipped in, 'What shared drive?'

Or they have a strategy no-one really buys into. I remember at a multinational company where I worked, the newish CEO presented his strategy that, to me, seemed clearly to be 'fixing yesterday's problems tomorrow'. I quit not long after.

Here are some further issues I see:

- The strategy is presented once a year, in a big roadshow, to the global CEO. This presentation takes the local executives weeks to prepare, while the CEO reviews it for two hours. It then doesn't get refreshed or tweaked for the rest of the year. It's lifeless.
- The strategy is retrofitted – as in the time I was asked to make a risky new product's revenue forecast be $800 million, exactly the shortfall predicted in other parts of the business.
- The strategy and budgeting are misaligned – for example, the budget is created based on previous years without taking into account the strategy.

Issues of delivery

After the leadership team meeting, many team members allocate nearly zero time in their diary to delivering their part in the agreed initiatives. Instead, they go back to focus almost exclusively on their functional area.

In a recent offsite, for example, I asked the team how much of their time they each spent on leadership team initiatives currently. They said 5 per cent. When I asked how much time they should spend, they said 20 per cent. That's a significant gap.

I also see the following issues:

- The leadership team is too big. At one company, 20 people would turn up to what was called the leadership team meeting. No decisions or even discussions were possible.
- Leadership team meetings are like a 'work-in-progress'. People show up to meetings unprepared. No decisions are made, or minutes taken. No-one takes the lead on owning the outcomes of meetings. The agenda is a random collection of unprioritised, short-term issues.
- The team cram strategic initiatives and short-term problems into the same meeting. The short-term issues take longer than expected to discuss, so the strategic initiatives fall off the agenda.
- Leadership team members don't delegate tasks or harness appropriate resources to deliver on the projects they are leading.
- No project reviews or post-mortems are undertaken.
- No-one with subject matter expertise is invited in to help solve problems. For example, I've seen a new IT project discussed by the leadership team without a technical expert present.

THE THREE TYPES OF INTELLIGENCE AND THE NINE BUILDING BLOCKS

Each of the three challenges – people, strategy and delivery – places distinctly different demands on a leadership team. And different types of skills and intelligence are required to meet these demands.

People and culture challenges require emotional skills

When relationship challenges exist within the leadership team, or broader organisation-wide culture issues, the leadership team will need to use its emotional intelligence to navigate these successfully.

Strategy challenges require critical thinking skills

Strategy planning requires leaders to understand complex systems and grapple with various options to steer the company through an evolving landscape. To meet these requirements, leaders need a range of critical thinking and problem-solving skills. I call this creative-analytical intelligence.

Delivery challenges require practical skills

Delivering on initiatives and turning all the talk into action requires a practical set of skills. In my experience, a specific intellectual ability is needed to close the gap between strategy and execution. I call this practical intelligence.

Each of these skills represents a different type of intelligence, as shown in table 2.1.

Table 2.1: The leadership team needs three types of intelligence

Type of intelligence	Represented by	And a state of
Practical Intelligence (PQ)	The team's hands	Doing
Creative-Analytical Intelligence (IQ)	The team's heads	Thinking
Emotional Intelligence (EQ)	The team's hearts	Being

These three types of intelligence are needed collectively by the team, so that it can become more intelligent than the sum of its parts.

One analogy for this is a hive of bees. Each of the bees on its own has limited knowledge and limited intelligence. Put them all together so they can communicate, compare notes and collaborate and they become a superorganism, capable of making collective decisions on where to forage (and even when to replace the queen – but that's a story for another time).

This collective intelligence is what you want for your leadership team – not just to allow each individual to flourish, but for the team collectively to reach heights they could not achieve alone.

The nine building blocks of team intelligence

In my model of collective intelligence, each type of intelligence has three building blocks within it, as shown in figure 2.1.

Figure 2.1: The nine building blocks of leadership team intelligence

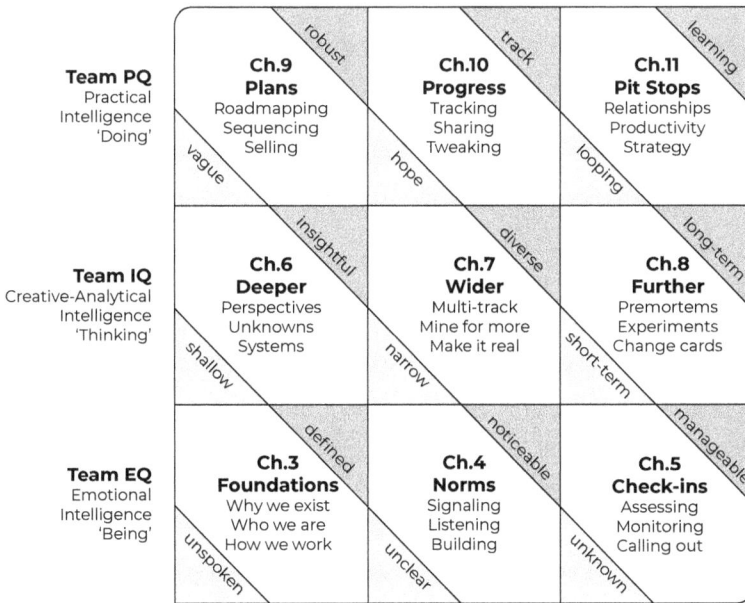

	Ch.9 Plans Roadmapping Sequencing Selling	Ch.10 Progress Tracking Sharing Tweaking	Ch.11 Pit Stops Relationships Productivity Strategy
Team PQ Practical Intelligence 'Doing'			
Team IQ Creative-Analytical Intelligence 'Thinking'	Ch.6 Deeper Perspectives Unknowns Systems	Ch.7 Wider Multi-track Mine for more Make it real	Ch.8 Further Premortems Experiments Change cards
Team EQ Emotional Intelligence 'Being'	Ch.3 Foundations Why we exist Who we are How we work	Ch.4 Norms Signaling Listening Building	Ch.5 Check-ins Assessing Monitoring Calling out

Each of these building blocks has its own self-contained chapter in this book. If you see a building block that grabs your attention, you can skip straight to that chapter.

Emotional intelligence is the topic of part II, with a chapter on each of the building blocks:

- the foundations of emotionally intelligent teams, and moving these from unspoken to defined
- behavioural norms for emotional intelligence, moving from unclear to noticeable
- check-ins to actively manage emotional intelligence, moving from unknown to manageable.

In part two, we look at creative-analytical intelligence and its three building blocks:

- thinking deeper to understand complex systems, and transforming this from shallow to inspirational
- thinking wider to generate more options, from narrow to diverse
- thinking further ahead to make better plans, from short term to long term.

In part three, we turn to practical intelligence, with chapters on:

- making plans, taking them from vague to robust
- tracking progress, moving away from hope and towards real results
- pit stops and post analysis, moving from looping to learning.

Measuring your team's collective intelligence

Before tackling the next three parts of this book, this is great place to pause and measure the current collective intelligence of your team. Your team can take the diagnostic survey I've created based on the three types of intelligence. You will receive a team intelligence report that breaks down each of the three types of intelligence into nine building blocks and 27 specific behaviours.

The diagnostic estimates your team's overall intelligence using a scale where 100 is the median, just like the classic IQ test. At the time of writing, the most intelligent team to take the test rated 124, and the lowest rated 72. To find out where your team sits today, go to robpyne.online/unlock.

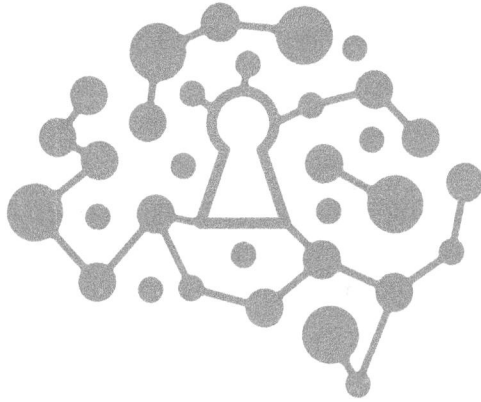

PART II

UNLOCKING THE TEAM'S
EMOTIONAL INTELLIGENCE

Do people cry in your leadership team meetings?

I imagine it's unusual, or even unheard of, in your team. But should it be like that? In late 2020, I ran a series of workshops where we encouraged leadership teams to open up about their high points, low points and turning points from the pandemic-affected year. In every workshop, someone shed a tear when they shared – or heard – stories of their pandemic trials. These stories included a whole range of emotional challenges, from being separated from partners, to teenage children struggling to cope, to illness.

If you are creating a leadership team that is a real team, not just a working group, you need to build emotional connections and bonds between the members.

That doesn't mean having people cry all the time, but it does mean you need to create an environment that allows for vulnerability and raises the group's emotional intelligence.

....

If leadership team members share the highs and lows of their year, their vulnerability builds trust and helps them get to know 'the person behind the colleague'.

....

ON AN EMOTIONAL KNIFE EDGE

We humans easily become defensive. In many different situations – if we think we hear a burglar downstairs at night, for example, or step into a networking event where we don't know anyone – we often raise our defences.

In work teams, including leadership teams, this defensiveness is not because we feel our physical safety is threatened. But we may feel our self-identity is threatened. We want to feel likeable, competent and significant in other people's eyes (see *Radical Collaboration* by James Tamm and Ronald Luyet for more on this). And any small behaviour on someone else's part can trigger our defences to go up.

We are all in the game of impression management. We do it so much, these actions are mainly subconscious.

We care what others think of us. In fact, 'not caring what other people think of me' is a symptom of being a psychopath. Ask yourself:

- What emotions did you experience about your contribution to your last leadership team meeting?
- What emotions did you have about other team members?
- What emotions did you have about the meeting as a whole?

It's probably easy for you to name a few emotions because we are all emotional creatures. We rarely feel neutral about ourselves or other people – or even meetings.

We care about how we're perceived. We care about whether people are on our side, or not on our side. We care what the team leader thinks about us. We care about the quality of meetings.

This care has a good side, creating motivation, passion, energy, drive and positivity.

And it has a dark side, increasing defensiveness, competitiveness, negativity, anxiety and fear.

You can develop the team's emotional intelligence so the group can spend more time on the good side – and self-correct when it ends up on the dark side.

BUILDING EMOTIONAL FOUNDATIONS

In the chapters in this part, I outline the three building blocks to unlocking the emotional intelligence of your leadership team. These three building blocks are designed to help you work with the emotions and feelings of the team. Feelings are a response, a reaction, to behaviours. This means:

- You need to be able to check in and see how people are feeling.
- Even better, you can create behavioural norms first.
- And, better still, you can help shape how the group sees itself: its frame. You can ask, 'Are we a real team?'

Chapter 3 explores the team's foundations – how the team perceives itself and what the team is for. One of the core concepts here is the difference between a working group and a real team.

In chapter 4, I cover *behavioural norms* – the rules team members learn. These norms include how to interact with each other, how to contribute and how to communicate. One of the fundamental principles here is *making each other feel heard*.

Chapter 5 then examines the potential of *check-ins* and *active emotional management* – covering how to help the team be self-aware and self-regulate. One of the ideas here is encouraging people to share their gut feel reactions, not hide them.

Building your team's emotional capital

If you create an environment where you have a real team, with emotionally intelligent behaviours and the ability to spot and self-correct problems, then you're building *emotional capital*.

Your investment creates a bank of trust, psychological safety and honesty.

And this will deliver returns in the form of greater resilience, more innovation, increased productivity and faster learning.

Building your organisation's Emotional Capital

The leadership team are often the leading players in role-modelling your organisation's values and behavioural norms.

Positive, emotionally intelligent behaviours in the leadership team will also go a long way to uphold and role-model the standards you want to see in other people.

This can happen in two ways: the leadership team can introduce emotionally intelligent behaviours into their functional teams in a cascade model, or they can extend the behaviours into their communications across the organisation.

....

Through building emotional intelligence, your leadership team can become the emotional beating heart of your company – or, if you like, The Emotional Capital.

....

CHOOSING YOUR FRAME

As Amy Edmondson outlines in *Teaming*, a cognitive frame is the 'set of assumptions and beliefs about a situation'.

Cognitive frames are usually hidden – even from ourselves.

When I watch my football team, Liverpool, play against Manchester United, I watch it with a set of assumptions and beliefs about Liverpool, and a set of not-so-positive assumptions about the opposition. A Manchester United supporter might as well be watching a different game, because their frame will be wildly different. Frames mean we see the world differently from each other.

But frames can be useful in the context of leadership teams because we can surface and share the assumptions and beliefs about what this leadership team is for, who is in it, and how it works.

Let's say you *don't* do this. Imagine a robust debate breaks out between two members and voices get raised.

One onlooker's frame may lead them to think, *At last; this is exactly what good leadership teams should do, because robust debate is important*. A second onlooker's frame, based on all their experiences, may lead them to think, *Oh my gosh. Both of them will never get promoted now; how painfully embarrassing for everyone*.

These frames affect *team* behaviours too, not just individuals' behaviours. In particular, Edmondson (quoting Dweck & Leggett's article 'A social cognitive approach to motivation and personality') recommends adopting a learning frame for your team instead of a performance frame:

> When people frame a task as a 'performance situation' they are more risk-averse and less willing to persist through obstacles than when the same task is framed as a 'learning situation'.

In the next chapter, I examine the foundations of an emotionally intelligent team as a way of creating a shared cognitive frame that promotes emotionally intelligent team behaviours.

3

Foundations.
The building blocks of team emotional intelligence.

A TEAM BUT NOT A TEAM

A few years into my career as a leadership team coach, the CEO of Venture Partners invited me to facilitate an offsite for two days in Fiji. The team turned out to be struggling to work well – for one specific reason.

The CEO was rumoured to be having a relationship with Irene, the corporate legal counsel. Everyone 'knew' about it, everyone talked about it, but it wasn't official – either for moral or legal reasons (many companies frown on senior leaders having internal relationships).

The situation was creating visible problems in the behaviours of Irene and the CEO. Irene seemed to be defensive about her position, and this occasionally flared into disruptive comments. But the CEO would not call her out on her behaviour.

Situations like this help us understand why emotional intelligence is so important – because we see what happens when we *don't* have it.

The consequences for the Venture Partners leadership team of not showing emotional intelligence were profound.

They weren't really a team. They weren't pursuing shared goals; they didn't have a strategy; they had as little to do with each other between meetings as possible; their discussions were centred on relatively low-value items such as the structure of the monthly all-staff meeting; and, of course, there was no trust in the room. So, when discussions went off on long tangents or became unproductive, no-one would intervene or call it out.

Examining the Venture Partners leadership team helps provide some further context to these chapters on emotional intelligence.

YOU MUST HAVE A SHARED UNDERSTANDING OF THE TEAM'S PURPOSE

The leadership team met for two days every other month and spent their time updating each other on their respective divisions and covering issues around centralised services such as legal and IT.

As far as I could tell (through various pre-briefing conversations), the members of this team regarded their meetings as painfully long, providing only 'listy' updates from their colleagues.

Company-wide strategy was not discussed, because strategy was devised at the divisional level. The parent company preferred to play a support role: providing central services, but not creating a strategy for the group as a whole.

Another feature was Brent, the CFO's right-hand man. Brent's exact title was not clear. He seldom spoke in meetings, and no-one seemed to know why he was there. But he did turn up to most, if not all, leadership team meetings. I'll come back to Brent later.

For now, let's focus on why this team even existed in the first place.

To uncover this, I'll expand on the approach I outlined in chapter 1, where I explored four ways leadership teams differ from other teams; that is, their:

- Purpose: *Why* does the team exist?
- People: *Who* is in the team?

- Product: *What* does the team produce?
- Process: *How* does the team operate?

In chapter 1, I used these four areas to differentiate leadership teams. They were *descriptions*.

In this chapter, we can use the questions as *prescriptions*, focusing in particular on why the team exists, who is in the team and how the team operates.

Answering these questions serves to help build a shared team identity. The answers serve as a frame for outlining the behaviours and norms of the team. They are the foundations of a team's emotional intelligence.

Knowing the answers to these questions allows people to understand how to behave in the team, and how to relate to others.

Self-identity: why does this team exist?

The opportunity cost of having a leadership team is high. Let's say you had ten people in your leadership team, with an average salary of $250,000. That means, for every one-day leadership team meeting, you could be burning the time-based equivalent of $37,500 (assuming that across your organisation, salaries are one third of revenue, so each leader should generate three times their salary in revenue). Meeting once a month adds up to an annualised opportunity cost approaching half a million dollars.

I'm putting a financial frame on this, helping you to sharpen the focus and ask, 'Why does this team exist?'

And this is precisely what I did with Venture Partners: I asked them to define what value they created as a leadership team, and for whom.

Their initial answers revealed that few people thought being in the team or having team meetings was of any value. It was a confronting – but necessary – realisation.

Many leadership team researchers support the importance of having a purpose, a 'why', for the team. In *Senior Leadership Teams: What it Takes to Make Them Great*, for example, authors Ruth

Wageman, Debra Nunes, James Burruss & Richard Hackman argue the essential pre-requisites for a team include clarity of purpose.

In Google's Project Aristotle, three of the predictors of team effectiveness were clarity ('how I contribute to success'), meaning ('finding a sense of purpose in work') and impact ('seeing my work make an impact').

And returning to Amy Edmondson in *Teaming*, she advises, 'leaders must communicate a clear and compelling purpose that resonates with all members of the team'.

In each case, and in my own experience, either explaining the team's purpose or having the team co-create its reason for being is shown to be vital. Framing this as 'what value do we create, and for whom?' takes the focus off a purely financial conversation and moves it into a dialogue about whom you are serving as the leadership team, and how you help them be successful.

Having this frame elevates the emotional meaning of the team and its goals.

Most teams, when asked these questions, define a stakeholder list similar to the following. Our stakeholders are:

· the owners of the business
· our employees
· our customers
· ourselves.

Interestingly, coming up with the fourth stakeholder on the list – ourselves – often takes them a little while longer. We can infer that many leadership team members don't think of the leadership team as a place for them to learn and grow.

Once you have this list of stakeholders, your team can then list what value you create *as a leadership team* for each group. An important distinction is that you're not focusing on the value each member creates in their functional 'head of' role; instead, you need to outline the value that the leadership team collectively creates. That's the value that wouldn't be realised if the leadership team were disbanded.

The value you create for each stakeholder groups could be as follows:

- For the owners of the business: we integrate the work across functions in service of a winning strategy.
- For our employees: we help make their jobs better and easier.
- For our customers: we ensure we stay close to customers' needs.
- For ourselves: we make sure we develop and grow individually through exposure to whole-of-business decisions.

When your team can create and prioritise this list of values, it creates an excellent foundation for discussing who should be on the team and how you should behave.

Having a shared sense of purpose is the first step in building an emotionally intelligent team, because it unites the team members around a meaningful reason for being.

Is it always possible to develop a purpose? Returning to the Venture Partners example, the team did not try to develop a sense of purpose that was strategic and dripping with meaning. They took a practical approach and realised they would best spend their time helping each other solve problems in small groups.

They now understood that they each valued the problem-solving smarts of the other leaders around the table, and they would be better served splitting off into groups of three or four for parts of their meeting. They'd still spend some time on whole group issues, and still hear updates from each division (now capped at ten minutes per person, timed by the CEO), but they'd also allocate time to solving real problems in small groups.

....
**Even teams with underlying dysfunctions can create value –
if you can facilitate honest dialogue.**
....

THE BOUNDARIES OF THE LEADERSHIP TEAM MUST BE CLEAR

How many people are in your leadership team?

This is a seemingly simple question, but answering it often ends up with people counting out loud – even when I'm on the phone talking to a leader, I can sense they are counting the people on their fingers.

One recent new client gave me different answers to this question as we planned their first leadership team offsite. It was four, then it was six, then it ended up as, 'five – one person also sits in on most leadership team meetings but isn't a member of the team'.

Building a real team with strong foundations requires 100 per cent clarity on who is in it – and who isn't.

Surprisingly, different team members may provide different answers – which is a direct signal they have different frames.

Being completely clear about who is on your leadership team is a second pre-requisite for an emotionally intelligent team. Feeling emotionally connected to a group of people is hard if they keep changing or it's unclear who is permanently on the team. Each team member needs to invest emotional energy building relation-ships with the other members, so they want to invest that wisely.

In Venture Partners, let's return to Brent – the right-hand man to the CFO who came to most leadership team meetings but didn't say anything. In theory, Brent's presence need make no difference to the effectiveness or emotional intelligence of the leadership team. In practice, it creates a sense of confusion and uncertainty that leaves everyone feeling less secure about the nature of this team, the strengths of this team, and even their role.

Team members want to know what Brent is there for, and if they are supposed to treat him as a team member or passenger.

Avoid having a Brent situation in your leadership team if you want to build strong foundations.

Setting clear boundaries

It's usually the team leader's job to outline who is in the team (and what they bring to the team). Exceptions to this rule do exist, especially when you become the leader and inherit an existing leadership team, or when you feel obligated to have a representa-tive from every business function.

Communication of the 'who' needs to reach both the team members themselves and the broader organisation. This can be done in concert with communicating a new strategy, a revitalised purpose for the leadership team, or refreshing the leadership team members.

However, this communication is often unclear, creating the level of uncertainty about who is actually part of the leadership team I discussed. Indeed, in *Senior Leadership Teams: What it Takes to Make Them Great*, researchers asked sixteen members of two different leadership teams how many people were in their leadership team.

Just five of the sixteen knew the right number of people.

....

All leadership team members need to be clear on who is on the team, not just the leader.

....

Now you have built two of the foundations for an emotionally intelligent team. You have created a shared understanding of why the team exists and who is in the team.

The last foundation is to agree on *how* this team operates.

HOW THE TEAM OPERATES MUST BE CLEAR

Professor Leigh Thompson of the Kellogg School of Management defines a team as follows:

> A team is a group of people who are interdependent with respect to information, resources, knowledge and skills and who seek to combine their efforts to achieve a common goal.

Emotional intelligence is necessary for successful teams to be interdependent, combine their efforts, and aim for a common goal.

Groups of people can come together without these features, but you may not want to call them a 'team' per se.

Venture Partners' leadership team wasn't really a team according to this frame, because they weren't interdependent and didn't have significant common goals. Moreover, each of their leadership team members would have felt a more substantial commitment and emotional connection to their division and functional leadership team. This lack of connection was exacerbated by their incentives being tied to the performance of their division, instead of the performance of the group as a whole.

In situations like this, having a leadership team may still be valuable, as long as there is a shared, realistic frame for what this team is for, how it creates value and how it behaves.

If your leadership team is anything like Venture Partners, your frame may also include calling it an 'executive committee' instead of a leadership team.

An executive committee (exco) is a working group, not a team, and a multitude of variations on these types of senior groups exist, including:

- the executive leadership team (ELT)
- the wider management team (WMT)
- the senior management team (SMT)
- the senior leadership group (SLG).

Of course, you may have adopted different names in your organisation. Note that the collective nouns include *committee*, *team* and *group*.

Committees and groups tend to be indicative of information sharing and co-ordination, whereas leadership teams should, in my view, include something more – where the collective has a significant responsibility to debate, make decisions, support each other and action joint projects.

The wider management teams and senior management teams I have encountered have tended to be more like working groups than teams.

Often an organisation attempts to manage a wide range of senior people through having two top teams. In my experience, many mid to large organisations I work with have an executive leadership team and a senior management team. Setting the boundaries for who is in which team can be simple, but working out the remit of both – and what the SMT in particular is for – turns out to be consistently troublesome.

Why is this? Primarily because the SMT doesn't get clear on its purpose, is often larger than a dozen people, doesn't do real shared work, and remains an information-sharing group rather than a real team. Members of the SMT become frustrated about the time the group takes up, and also disappointed they get no real upwards input into decisions and strategy.

Are you a real team?

....

Having leadership team meetings isn't the same as being a leadership team.

....

I first heard this from ex–Richmond Tigers CEO – turned leadership coach – Cameron Schwab.

Around the same time, I'd been talking to a CEO about her leadership team. I'd asked some typical questions: 'Who's in the team? How does it work? How often do you meet?'

After she answered the questions, I shared some of my work on leadership team intelligence. She soon realised her team wasn't really a team – in fact, it wasn't very 'teamy' at all. She used meetings simply to share updates and delegate work to her direct reports.

The emotional intelligence of her leadership group would likely have been low. Her direct reports may have felt communication in meetings only went one way, and their voices and ideas weren't being heard.

In such situations, group members feel limited connection to the other group members, and they have no interdependencies.

These aspects of being a real team are the third required element of an emotionally intelligent team. They represent a sense of belonging in the following ways:

· Belonging to a team that has my back.
· Belonging to a team who are building something meaningful together.
· Belonging to a team who help each other.

One team I worked with developed an idea to ensure they each had other's backs: they called it answering the 'bat call' (based on the Bat-Signal from the original Batman series, used by the Gotham City Police Department so Batman could come flying in to save the day).

This team's bat call acknowledged that the group valued support between meetings, but a straightforward and easy way to ask for it hadn't existed. And as a result, they had rarely discussed problems between meetings. Now, when one team member issued a bat call – or a request for support – other team members made sure they answered it.

Other ways to create a 'real team' with team members who support each other between meetings include:

- establishing a specific channel for the leadership team to communicate and stay connected – for example, using your internal 'chat' system
- co-locating to create opportunities to bump into each other – for example, considering how Steve Jobs designed the Pixar headquarters to optimise spontaneous meetings (as outlined in *The Innovators: How a Group of Hackers, Geniuses, and Geeks Created the Digital Revolution* by Walter Isaacson)
- providing lunch in the office once or twice a week for the leaders, or everyone
- establishing peer coaching pairs, where two members of the team meet regularly to coach each other through challenges.

Asking for support is both a *signal* of emotionally intelligent teams, and a behaviour that will *create* more emotional intelligence. Asking for help creates mutual dependence and opportunities to do real work. It also builds trust.

As you'll discover in the following chapter, however, it's not just the asking that counts but also how the other team members respond. Do they come running? Or do they assume someone else will help out, and keep going on their path?

Being a real team doesn't mean doing 'trust falls' into each other's arms with a blindfold on; it doesn't mean becoming best friends; and it doesn't necessarily mean you need to be co-located.

It *does* mean creating an environment where people can feel, 'This is my A-team. If I need help, I can call on this group. We do real work together. We have strong foundations.'

All of this gives the group a shared frame, which is the foundation of an emotionally intelligent team.

Chapter summary

Building solid foundations for your team requires three things:

- First, establishing why the team exists – what value does it create and for whom?
- Second, establishing who is on the team – defining team members and why they are included.
- Third, making sure this a real interdependent team where team members support each other as individuals.

Take action

To build your emotionally intelligent foundations:

- Create a shared team purpose by establishing what value you create for which stakeholders.
- Eliminate any confusion around who's in the team; build a communication plan so the wider organisation gets to know who's in the team and what you're focused on.
- Find ways to support each other between meetings, such as the issuing – and answering – of the 'bat call'.

Next

Once you've built your foundations, you can turn to developing behavioural norms. And then you'll need ways of managing emotions in real time. I cover these in the next two chapters.

4

Norms.
The behaviours of emotionally intelligent teams.

EMOTIONAL INTELLIGENCE REQUIRES SIGNALLING

Qcorp is a logistics business going through significant transformation. Its Operations leadership team has several new members – including the head of operations, Brian. The team also has four members who have been there for several years, and Brian inherited these people in his leadership team.

One of these inherited people was Rachel.

At a leadership team offsite meeting, the team was reviewing their last quarter, and each member was given the opportunity to share the successes and failures in their area.

When it came to Rachel's turn, she weighed up her options, and then jumped in. She decided to be vulnerable. She shared some of her challenges in managing her team of ten, many of whom were demotivated and not on board with the company's transformation plans. She admitted losing confidence in her leadership skills. She was on the verge of tears in front of her teammates.

What happened next?

Before I reveal the ending, let's take a look at some current research on vulnerability.

Vulnerability is one of the best ways to build trust, according to Patrick Lencioni, author of best seller *The Five Dysfunctions of a Team*. Being vulnerable signals, 'I'm sharing something with you that might make me look less-than-perfect. I'm trusting you not to misuse that knowledge or hold it against me.'

Signals of vulnerability can release the chemical oxytocin into the brains of both parties. And as neuroeconomist Dr Paul Zak, author of *Trust Factor*, has shown, when your brain releases oxytocin, it reduces the fear of trusting others – even strangers.

However, Jeff Polzer, a professor in organisational behaviour at Harvard, showed that expressing vulnerability only builds trust if the listener signals their empathy and support in return.

He calls this a 'vulnerability loop', and an example would be as follows:

1. Anna shares with Ben something that makes her feel vulnerable.
2. Ben signals he has recognised her vulnerability – with body language (a nod, smile) or with his own expression of vulnerability and empathy.
3. Anna picks up on Ben's reciprocal signal.
4. Anna and Ben have created some shared empathy, which can help build trust.

Back to Rachel and Brian at Qcorp.

Rachel had bravely taken step one by opening up and being vulnerable to her leadership team.

For this show of vulnerability to work, the team – particularly Brian – needed to signal recognition and empathy.

That's not what Brian did. After a lengthy and uncomfortable silence, during which another team member passed the tissues to Rachel, Brian rattled off some rational reasons why Rachel's points weren't valid. His response was along the lines of, 'That's not right, Rachel. You just need to tell your team they need to get on board.'

Brian was attempting to be supportive, but his comments lacked empathy and did not signal recognition or reciprocity.

Indeed, this response was in line with my findings for the Qcorp team, based on my Team Intelligence Diagnostic – which showed the team had a below-average emotional intelligence rating.

You can imagine the other team members would have felt very awkward during this exchange and might have resolved in their minds never to open up and be vulnerable.

Unless this can be addressed, the team will continue to have low trust, and this will hold back the organisation. As Dr Paul Zak showed in 'The Neuroscience of Trust':

> Compared with people at low-trust companies, people at high-trust companies report: 74% less stress, 106% more energy at work, 50% higher productivity, 13% fewer sick days, 76% more engagement, 29% more satisfaction with their lives, 40% less burnout.

Along with the research, this real example from Qcorp shows the importance of building trust, and the opportunities (and risks) that come from being vulnerable. And it highlights the way vulnerability requires a loop – trust builds when the signals are reciprocated.

In this chapter, I explore the signals and behavioural norms for leadership teams that help the team be more productive and solve problems better.

SIGNALS THAT HELP OTHERS FEEL LIKED, COMPETENT AND SIGNIFICANT

To build an emotionally intelligent team, you need to encourage emotionally intelligent behaviours and make these the norm in your leadership team interactions.

At the core of emotionally intelligent behaviour is making signals that help other team members feel three things:

1. We all want to feel liked.
2. We all want to feel competent.
3. We all want to feel significant.

These three drivers are deep-seated social needs. (For more in this area see, for example, Jim Tamm and Ronald Luyet's *Radical Collaboration*.)

As a leader, you can be proactive in how you make these signals – keeping in mind that your behaviour is particularly important for two reasons.

First, people want to feel liked, competent, and significant in your eyes because you have the highest status and have control of how their career progresses.

Second, you are also the role model, providing behavioural cues for others to follow, and therefore for the group to create norms.

As already outlined, Professor Jeff Polzer showed that reciprocating vulnerability is one signal to build trust and improve performance. Dr Zak also revealed several other signals that build trust according to his experiments and surveys. These behaviours are:

- *Recognise excellence:* Recognise good work quickly, unexpectedly and publicly.
- *Assign challenging but achievable tasks:* A moderate level of stress – not too little, not too much – helps release oxytocin and other neurochemicals that increase focus and strengthen social connections.
- *Trust people to do things their way:* It's motivating to be given a little more control and freedom. (For more on this, see *Drive* by Dan Pink.)
- *Share information broadly:* Zak suggests 'uncertainty about the company's direction leads to chronic stress, which inhibits the release of oxytocin and undermines teamwork'. So leaders need to demonstrate the behaviour of sharing information. (I return to this topic in chapters 10 and 11, where I explore planning and progress.)
- *Intentionally build relationships:* In 'The neurobiology of collective action', Zak and co-author Jorge Barraza showed how team performance improves when people go out of their way to build social relationships with other team members. This is not always the norm in organisations, especially when leadership team meetings focus exclusively on work issues and problems.

- *Encourage whole-person growth:* Trust is built when you encourage your team members to make progress on their overall growth as a person *and* in their work-related skills.

If these behaviours become norms in your leadership team, you will also increase emotional intelligence and create emotional capital.

Zak's evidence links these behaviours to increases in engagement (+76 per cent) and productivity (+50 per cent).

But what emotionally intelligent behaviours also promote better problem-solving? As leadership teams have a much-increased need to do great thinking as well as be motivated and productive, this is an important question – and one that is considered in the next section.

SIGNALS THAT UNLOCK THE TEAM'S CREATIVE-ANALYTICAL INTELLIGENCE

In 2010, five researchers set out to understand the collective intelligence of teams. Experts have known for many years that *individuals* have a generalised intelligence called factor G. A person who is good at solving numerical puzzles, for example, is also likely to be above average on solving puzzles that use words or spatial arrangements – in this case, their general intelligence crosses these domains.

The research into the collective intelligence of teams, led by Anita Williams Woolley and published in 2010, set out to discover if this crossover is also true with teams – that is, whether they have a generalised intelligence from one problem-solving task to another. They subjected teams of people to hours of tests and looked at their intelligence across disparate tasks – from brainstorming to moral judgements, and from negotiation to critical thinking.

The results are important for how we think about teams in our organisations. First, they found that, just like individuals, teams do have this collective, generalised intelligence, which they came to call 'factor C'. If a team was collectively good at the brainstorming task, they tended to be better in negotiating tasks and so on.

Factor C is the property you want to build in your leadership team, so the team is more successful at critical, creative and analytical thinking – and, ultimately, at solving problems and developing winning strategies.

....

Collective intelligence is an emergent property

In a fascinating twist, the researchers found a *team's* IQ (factor C in their language) is not highly related to the team members' individual IQ ratings.

In MIT senior lecturer Peter Senge's words in *The Fifth Discipline*,

> How can a team of committed managers with individual IQs above 120 have a collective IQ of 63?

Woolley and her team found two emotionally intelligent behaviours in the team led to higher Team IQ. These are emergent properties of the team, and come from the dynamics between members. It's the team's emotional behaviours – and signals – which make it smarter than the sum of its parts.

Social sensitivity

The single most significant predictor of a team's mental performance on these tough challenges was their members' social sensitivity. To understand precisely what this is, consider the test they use to measure it: the 'Reading the mind in the eyes' test. (If you search for it online, you can take the test yourself.) The test asks you to look at about 40 different pairs of eyes and interpret how each person feels, picking from four options each time.

If individuals in a team do well on this test – understanding how other people are feeling just by looking in their eyes – the team will be better at solving challenging problems, on average.

How does social sensitivity improve a team's mental performance? Research from Woolley and her colleagues indicates that higher social sensitivity benefits the team's intelligence in several ways. First of all, benefits emerge in brainstorming, where ideas are being discussed. People with higher social sensitivity are more flexible thinkers, and they're better at perceiving and responding to input from others.

A level of trust also comes from social sensitivity, where people are seen as dependable and sharing the burden of work. When good social sensitivity exists, the team produces high-quality work, communication is effective, and people are respectful to each other and able to compromise where needed.

Conversational turn-taking

The researchers found the C Factor was higher if there was *equality of conversational turn-taking* – that is, does everyone have equal airtime? If, over the course of the leadership team meeting, everyone speaks for a roughly equal amount of time, it leads to better team problem-solving performance.

You're probably familiar with those meetings and teams where one or two people dominate the talking. Those teams are decreasing their chances of finding the best solution because they only hear one or two voices.

The role of gender

A high correlation also emerged between Factor C and the number of females in the team – that is, the more females in the team, the higher the collective intelligence of the group. Women, it seems, are generally better at the social dynamics needed to help solve challenging problems. In fact, the most intelligent type of team in the study was a team that was almost all females, with just one male.

Social sensitivity and turn-taking allow the team to build on each other's ideas and cooperate non-defensively.

THE VALUE OF EMOTIONALLY INTELLIGENT BEHAVIOURS

The research from Zak, Polzer and Woolley shows that emotionally intelligent behaviours have many positive outcomes.

If you create an environment where people feel liked, competent and significant, and help people develop trusting relationships, they will be more engaged, motivated and productive.

And they will be better at surfacing the collective intelligence of the group to solve challenging problems.

This behaviour isn't about being nice for the sake of it. It's not about high fives and teamy clichés – such as, 'Together everyone achieves more!' The evidence simply backs up what we know in our hearts already.

....

Investing in how the team behaves will pay a significant dividend in increased emotional capital, and will improve the team's results.

....

The following sections explore the behaviours to encourage, and the behaviours to avoid.

Watch out for false consensus

One specific risk in focusing on emotional intelligence is 'false consensus'.

Amy Edmondson's work on psychological safety in *The Fearless Organization* includes a useful guide to the difference between real and false consensus.

Edmondson shows that people at work are naturally defensive and worried about how they come across to their colleagues. This can lead to leadership team meetings where people nod and agree, but stay silent about their real concerns, fearing they may be judged or punished if they offer a dissenting view.

The result is a false consensus – and it can be dangerous, because it can lead to a lack of commitment and follow-up to the team's decisions. Team members feel unheard – even though they've been asked, 'Is everyone okay with this?'

Leaders often feel frustrated by this false consensus. People don't speak up. Most of the conversation comes from a small number of people. The others offer little resistance. The leader expects people to speak up. However, if the team does not have a level of trust, team members feel speaking up is risky.

On the surface, a team like this can look highly functional. Meetings are quicker and debate easier because there are fewer voices. Consensus is reached.

In reality, the consensus is false. The commitment is low. And little comes from these agreements.

If you fear you may have a team like this, which lacks 'psychological safety', you need to work on the signals you give out. And the team's norms need to change.

You can start by encouraging the loud people to listen more. Encourage and reward the quieter people for speaking up. Recognise their contribution. Thank them for raising good questions. Over time, you will develop a team with real debate and dialogue. False consensus will become a memory.

The leader's role is to recognise the importance of emotional intelligence, role-model emotionally intelligent behaviours, and send out clear signals to reward appropriate behaviours from your team.

Listen with empathy to make people feel heard

Emotionally intelligent behaviours are focused on communication between members of the leadership team. We've looked at *signalling* your recognition and empathy, and we've looked at *equality of conversational turn-taking*.

To get the most out of the team members' collective intelligence, the skill of listening needs to be an additional focus.

You *listen* and then signal recognition and empathy.

You *listen* and then you make a contribution that adds to the previous one.

If seven people are in your leadership team, you will on average spend 14 per cent of the group's discussion time talking, and around 86 per cent listening.

And yet, leaders focus much more on improving their 'communication output' skills: how to present and communicate ideas.

Models of listening skills tend to differentiate between levels of listening. Considering models from experts such as Oscar Trimboli (author of *Deep Listening: Impact Beyond Words*) and Melissa Daimler (author of *Harvard Business Review* article 'Listening is an overlooked leadership tool') provides an outline of these levels:

- Level 1: Listening for a gap to speak – being minimally polite.
- Level 2: Listening to the content – acknowledging their words.
- Level 3: Listening to the context – what's unsaid, what does it mean?
- Level 4: Listening to the connections – how does this connect to other ideas?

Listening on its own is not enough. You need to *signal* you're listening. Some call this active listening. I prefer to call it 'making people feel heard', because this reminds you to exhibit your attention. This includes using your body language, paraphrasing, questioning, repeating their language and building on their point. All are skills of good listeners who make their conversational partners feel heard – and that makes them feel significant, competent and likeable.

Listening isn't just a set of skills, however. It's a mindset.

In my experience, it's hard to be a better listener if you don't believe most of the following:

- *Humility: 'Might I be wrong?'* If you are routinely confident in your ideas, you may unconsciously become a less skilled listener. The best leaders I've worked with have a level of humility – and vulnerability – about their skills and opinions. Evidence included in the *Leadership Quarterly* article 'How leader humility helps teams to be humbler, psychologically stronger, and more effective' suggests leaders who express humility improve the team's performance by fostering greater learning in the team and improving team communication.
- *Respect: 'My teammates have valuable contributions'* As the saying goes, 'If you are the smartest person in the room, you're in the wrong room'. As a leader, you may have concluded – consciously or subconsciously – that certain members of your team have less important contributions to make when problem-solving. It is easy to frame this as *their* problem. However, it can be reframed as an opportunity for you as the leader to coach, encourage their contributions, or make better use of their skills

within the leadership team. If you are the smartest person in the room, is it possible you haven't attracted the right level of talent into your leadership team?

- *Curiosity: 'I wonder if other ideas or perspectives are possible?'* In any leadership team, there tend to be times when we use divergent thinking to listen to a variety of perspectives. And there are other times when we use convergent thinking to prioritise, align and make decisions. According to Juliet Bourke's *Which Two Heads are Better Than One?,* most leaders have a thinking style that tends toward convergence – meaning they are outcome-focused, asking, 'What are we trying to achieve, and how will we get there?' If this is you, you'll find yourself wanting to limit the time spent in divergent thinking. You may find it frustrating when people introduce new perspectives. You probably find yourself directing the meeting and, as a result, being less open to listening to new ideas and perspectives – when the opposite may be needed.

Some simple ideas to improve your listening

You can use the rule 'Leaders listen first and speak last' to remind you to stop and listen before offering your point of view.

This also has the benefit of reducing groupthink. Often the leader shares their views early and, due to the leader's status – sometimes compounded by a lack of psychological safety – other team members are less likely to offer divergent views. Consensus ensues.

Other simple ways to listen better and make people feel heard more include:

- Use your body language to make eye contact, angle your whole body towards the person speaking, and put your smartphone down.
- Ask more varied questions. For example, ask about feelings, not just facts – 'How do you feel about this issue?' Question assumptions – 'Tell me more about how you reached that conclusion?'
- Paraphrase and build on others' contributions.
- Acknowledge their contribution when you add your point of view.
- Encourage the quieter team members by asking for and acknowledging their contribution.

When you need to listen less

There are limits to how much listening you can or should do. Three situations are essential to recognise and avoid.

The go-around

Ensuring equality of conversational turn-taking could be interpreted as implementing a simple rule, 'Ask every team member for their contribution on every agenda item'. A moment's consideration will reveal this to be unworkable and unwise, however, especially when you have a larger leadership team of seven or more people. There is a point of diminishing returns, where extra points of view are increasingly less likely to add real value to the discussion.

To avoid this, you can canvass the subject matter experts first, and then ask the other team members for questions, perhaps singling out one or two for their specific contributions.

Over time, make sure you regularly hear from everyone, but not on every issue. Don't make the Head of HR comment on marketing, IT *and* finance problems, but encourage them to contribute questions or perspectives to one or two of these areas.

The non-expert

Weighing the contributions of your team according to their subject matter expertise is essential. However, you can encourage your other team members' broader perspectives and questions to allow them to make a valuable contribution.

The head of sales might not know much about IT infrastructure, but they should be allowed to contribute questions – for example, about the expected outcomes, risk factors, timings and success measurements for a new project.

The loudest voice

In my experience, the majority of teams have a loud person. Usually, that loudest voice makes valuable contributions. But there are limits – hearing from them for the fourth time on the same topic is less valuable than hearing another voice.

If you face this situation, the rest of the leadership team are looking to you to deal with it.

Here are two techniques to deal with the loud person:

1. *Use your body language*. When the loud person speaks, move your eyes and turn your whole body towards another, quieter person and then, at an appropriate moment, ask for their contribution.
2. *Make sure the loud person feels heard by explicitly telling them so.* Send a loud signal: 'Thanks Frank, I heard you have some reservations about the infrastructure project and see some substantial risks to our most important customer accounts. Now I'd like to hear some other perspectives. Clare?'

BUILD ON OTHER PEOPLE'S CONTRIBUTIONS THROUGH DIALOGUE

The behavioural norms outlined in the previous sections help a team be more productive and solve problems better.

One more behavioural approach is designed to help a team be smarter than the sum of its parts. It's called dialogue, and it is a surprisingly rare form of conversation.

Defining dialogue

We can define dialogue by comparing it with its opposite: debate.

Debate is *competitive thinking*. Individuals put forward their ideas and advocate for them. The best idea wins – in theory. It is a zero-sum game, with one winner, and everyone else loses. This is the type of thinking we see from lawyers: marshalling the evidence to fit an existing position, and competing for who wins in court. Leadership team meetings often resemble this – in structure, if not in tone. If they act like this, they are the sum of their parts, and they cannot be more than the sum of their parts.

....
Dialogue is collective thinking.
Debate is competitive thinking.
....

The group does not advocate. They leave their preconceptions at the door and are driven to find the best answers together. This is a positive-sum game where your idea can unlock a new idea in me. We can be more than the sum of our parts. We can create ideas that are better than any of us could have produced alone. This is sometimes called 'appreciative inquiry', represented by the concept of a group of detectives in an incident room trying to work together to find the truth, not looking to marshal evidence against a suspect, and not competing with each other.

Why dialogue is rare

The evolution of legal thinking, political discourse and the scientific method have prioritised competitive thinking over collective thinking. Debate has come to the fore. Advocacy has trumped inquiry.

You can see this in many areas – for example, the confirmation hearings for Supreme Court justices in the United States.

Although dialogue has its roots in Ancient Greece, it has ceded ground to a Western style of individualism that promotes the power of individual genius.

However, now that the systems and businesses we operate in have reached a level of complexity that surpasses any individual's understanding, we need to promote the resurgence of dialogue in our leadership teams.

The features of dialogue

In *On Dialogue*, David Bohm suggests the following features of a productive dialogue:

- Each participant must suspend their assumptions.
- All participants must regard one another as teammates, in a collective search for truth.
- A 'facilitator' is needed, who keeps the dialogue on track and maintains the context.

These features build on the emotionally intelligent behaviours outlined through this chapter.

'Suspending your assumptions' is the same as being clear on your frame or perspective. It requires you to open up, be vulnerable and be open. In fact, it requires a learning frame as espoused by Amy Edmondson in her work on psychological safety.

'Regarding each other as colleagues' draws on equality, turn-taking and trust.

And your role as leader is to 'facilitate' the dialogue, not pass judgement. To listen and make people feel heard.

One of the results of dialogue is that the winning idea belongs to everyone. At the end of a dialogue, a resolution is reached and no-one can remember whose idea it was originally.

It's collective thinking, not competitive thinking.

How to build dialogue into your leadership team discussions

The leadership team at Trackcity decided they needed to strengthen their organisation's culture, which had been diluted as they'd grown from five people to 300 people.

They wanted to sharpen up their team values so that the culture could be more engaging, more productive and more innovative.

Leadership teams often tackle such a project with a brainstorm and a robust debate before settling on a set of values acceptable to each member of the team.

Trackcity took a different approach: the team decided to collectively search for the truth. What really were their values?

At 10 am one day in December, they had their teams in every market stop work for 30 minutes and come together to contribute their ideas about the best of Trackcity. Each person was asked to answer one of several questions including:

- *What was your best day at Trackcity and why?*
- *Who represents the best of Trackcity and why?*

They created a kind of relay across seven time zones, with each office recording a video of responses and sending it to the next office – first New Zealand, then Australia, then the UK and South Africa, and then the US and Canada.

The full contributions of 300 people were gathered and shared with the leadership team a few days later. They divided up the stories. Each read a stack and took notes on the themes they could see.

Then they wrote the themes on sticky notes and stuck them to the wall.

(At this point, perhaps you can see they've conducted the kind of appreciative inquiry discussed earlier in this chapter, working together to discern the truth: what are our values, based on the best experiences of our staff?)

Dialogue began next as the leadership team worked together to turn 300 real stories into a set of authentic and motivating values.

First, the team had to discuss what a good set of values would look like. Then, they needed to find the strongest themes in the 300 stories to co-create a workable set of values that met the criteria.

They also collected the stories and grouped exemplars for each of the values. This was turned into a book to support the 'launch' of the values.

This Trackcity example resulted in a set of values still in active use four years later. The process of appreciative enquiry and dialogue was new to this team and produced outstanding results. Why? They created:

- a *collective search for the truth* – similar to detectives in an incident room looking through evidence and discovering patterns.
- an explicit dialogue about what makes a good set of values, so they could create the *frame* together.

The process for Trackcity also required two facilitators to hold the context and keep the dialogue on track. The facilitators made sure the behavioural norms allowed this team's emotional intelligence to flourish and led to an effective solution to the question at hand.

The second advantage of facilitators is they can help you capture the thinking as you go, making it easier to build on each other's contributions, like adding bricks to a wall.

Dialogue is not the only approach a leadership team should take. There is lots of space to maintain a debate-style conversation, and that can still be effective if you pay attention to emotionally intelligent behaviours and signals.

However, dialogue works well with emotional intelligence and is ideal for building a team smarter than the sum of its parts. Debate plays to individual egos more, rewarding individual excellence and advocacy. This approach has become the primary approach to leadership discussions. I think it's time to turn some of these debates into dialogues.

Chapter summary

Every team has unwritten rules on what's acceptable. But these can be quite loose and inconsistent. Effective leadership teams have emotionally intelligent behavioural norms that bring out the best from each team member. These include signalling so others feel liked, competent and significant; listening to build on others' comments; and engaging in dialogue as well as debate.

Take action

Here's how you can implement beneficial behavioural norms:

- Identify the emotionally intelligent behaviours you want to promote, based on the evidence and your own experience.
- Set clear behavioural expectations and role-model these behaviours.
- Signal your recognition and empathy when you see people being open and vulnerable.
- Remember leaders listen first and speak last.

- Develop a listening mindset (showing humility, respect and curiosity) and make people feel heard.
- Learn to manage the loud person with your body language and making them feel heard.
- Build your team's skills in dialogue and appreciative enquiry – and you'll find your team EQ will increase.

Next

Rules and norms are there to be broken. In the next chapter, I explore how to actively manage the team's emotions and how to call out unhelpful behaviours when you see them.

5

Check-ins.
Actively managing the team's emotions.

CHECK IN YOUR BAGGAGE

An hour into a leadership offsite with Westcorp, I noticed several long faces and tired body language as we tried to move up the mental gears to discuss next year's strategy.

The team was at the tail end of a tough year. Several significant customers had been lost. The longstanding CEO had departed, and a new one arrived. They'd been trying to rescue the year with an intensive new business program, which had been exhausting. Several team members had been asked to retrench some of their direct reports.

They had baggage.

I called a break, and when we returned, I ran a quick emotional check-in, and a few people admitted they were struggling to move through the mental gears. So, we ran an exercise called 'check in your baggage'. I asked them to draw a picture of a suitcase and then write inside it the answer to, 'What is holding you back today?'

I asked them to consider what about the past was causing them to struggle with the future. I then asked them to pick one colleague and share their baggage. Then I invited them to either be vulnerable and share their baggage with the whole group, or simply 'check in their baggage' and leave the piece of paper outside the room for the day.

This intervention turned around the team's mood and energy and allowed the team to work together to create an annual strategy.

This short example includes two specific approaches to actively managing the group's emotional intelligence.

First, the problem must be spotted and acknowledged by the group.

Second, work needs to be paused while you directly address it.

Then, the team can get back to work.

If I hadn't intervened, we would have struggled the entire day and ended up with a strategy few people were committed to. The team would have left the workshop less aligned and more frustrated.

....
Leadership teams can develop emotional baggage over time, or issues can suddenly flare up. In either case, the team will be better off if any baggage is declared and left at the door.
....

Addressing baggage requires an *active* approach to managing emotional intelligence in the team.

Once you've built the foundations for emotional intelligence and established behavioural norms, you can take four main steps to manage the team's emotions actively:

1. Check in with each team member's wellbeing every meeting.
2. Monitor the emotional temperature during tricky discussions.
3. Call out destructive behaviours – in constructive ways.
4. Assess the team's emotional capital every quarter.

It's likely you already do some of the preceding steps as a leader. You may also see opportunities to improve the way you lead, and better role-model these steps.

In the following sections in this chapter, I explore each of these steps in more detail.

CHECK IN WITH THE TEAM AT THE START OF MEETINGS

Many leaders are members of organisations such as The Executive Connection (TEC), based in Sydney, Australia. In these organisations, leaders get together with other leaders from different companies to discuss their challenges and learn from each other. A chair leads the monthly meeting.

In one such meeting I attended (as an external speaker), the chair took the emotional temperature of everyone in the room. He drew a vertical line on a whiteboard and then asked each member to share how they'd rate their life out of ten, and how they'd rate their work out of ten.

These CEOs dedicated the first half-hour of their meeting to this temperature checking and sharing.

Many of them shared family issues. One had a son who'd been in trouble for shoplifting. Another was going through a divorce. A third was facing significant problems with their business partner.

I was struck with how a group of CEOs would dedicate a significant proportion of their valuable time to what some might see as small talk. And then I realised this, of course, wasn't small talk at all. It was 'big talk': bravely sharing their real issues, being vulnerable, seeing the person behind the colleague.

This 'temperature check' process was formulated to turn this group of CEOs into something more than a monthly meeting. Could they instead become mutual support for each other?

Five reasons to check in

Dedicating time to checking in on life and work sends a *signal* to your team that you value them as a person, not just a colleague.

It promotes mutual *support*. If you're having an issue, can we help pick up the slack for you?

It triggers empathy and *social sensitivity*. This can reduce conflict over work issues later in the meeting.

It builds a *real team* instead of just a working group. It gives a sense of belonging.

It is *intentional relationship building*, which is essential and much more effective than relying on relationships to naturally form between people who often don't see each other between meetings.

Further evidence supporting check-ins and active emotional management

Smaranda Boroş, Professor of Intercultural Management and Organisational Behaviour at Vlerick Business School in Belgium, has studied how teams can improve their emotional intelligence.

In an experiment run with Delia Vîrgă, Boroş looked at teams tackling a challenging task. Half the teams received six extra guidelines to help the group run smoothly:

1. Have a 'check-in' at the beginning of the meeting – that is, ask how everyone is doing.
2. Assume that undesirable behaviour takes place for a reason. Find out what the reason is. Ask questions and listen. Avoid negative attributions.
3. As the work proceeds, tell your teammates what you are thinking and how you are feeling about the process.
4. When you make decisions, ask whether everyone agrees with the decision.
5. Question the quickness of taking a decision.
6. Ask quiet members what they think.

Teams who received the guidelines found it easier to resolve conflicts quickly and maintain motivation. This worked especially well for teams who started with low emotional intelligence.

Boroş and Vîrgă also recommended adding a 'review-and-reflect' moment at the end of longer tasks – asking, for example, 'How was the atmosphere today? How was our energy? Do we need to change anything?'

Such experiments are often run with university students working on artificial problem-solving tasks. How can you interpret them for your leadership team?

MONITOR THE EMOTIONAL TEMPERATURE DURING MEETINGS

I once ran a strategy workshop with four 'frenemies'.

The CEOs of four competing companies came together to fund a marketing campaign to grow their category. I was asked to facilitate their meetings to decide on their joint marketing strategy.

This was a group of successful, highly competitive entrepreneurs. There promised to be an undercurrent of emotions beneath the surface.

In situations like this, business leaders rarely state their feelings. Instead, they hide their feelings behind their considered comments and contributions.

This tendency can create problems. Our initial 'gut feel' emotional reactions to someone else's idea are not separate from our subsequent considered comments. The gut feel reactions *drive* our considered comments.

Evidence of this causation comes from Daniel Kahneman, Nobel Prize winning behavioural economist. In his bestseller *Thinking, Fast and Slow*, he outlines two systems in our brain. The fast one, which Kahneman calls 'System 1', makes instant decisions, subconsciously making assessments that surface in our brains as a feeling, based on the question do we like this idea or not? The slow one, which Kahneman calls 'System 2', is where we think consciously about an issue, hold the concepts in our mind and make conscious decisions.

Kahneman's extensive research revealed that System 2 often plays the role of post-rationalising System 1's decision.

....
Your conscious thinking merely acts to justify your gut feel.
....

If you are presented with an idea, you immediately get a gut feel for it. Then your conscious brain goes to work trying to work out why you do or don't like it. Then you open your mouth and make some considered comment about the strategic benefits or risks of the idea.

This leads to people developing competing arguments to support their gut feel. It becomes a debate. Not just that, but a debate that is *secretly* based on various people's gut feel and emotional reactions.

Surfacing the feelings under the facts

Drawing on the concept of dialogue, the solution to this rationalisation of gut feel reactions is for everyone to hold up their assumptions for the others to see. In simpler words, why not share your gut feel before you then move to more rational thinking?

This is not a new idea. Edward de Bono's *Six Hats Thinking*, which we'll encounter in more detail in chapter 6, encourages the team to sometimes use red hat thinking, where you simply state your gut feel – your emotional reaction to the idea.

This is the technique I used with the four frenemies. When an idea was tabled, they each shared their 'emotional reaction' in turn around the table. We wrote these down and then moved to assess each idea's pros and cons in a more 'rational' discussion.

Leadership teams often find this process refreshing. But some also struggle with it. Typically, when we ask a team about their emotional reactions, I prompt them to use emotional words. And yet they often revert to more rational expressions, such as 'The logo is too big.' Truly expressing emotional responses requires a little practice and careful facilitation.

This approach is a specific and structured application of tip number three from Boroş and Vîrgă: 'As the work proceeds, tell your teammates what you are thinking and how you are feeling about the process.'

Avoiding emotional explosions

With the four frenemies, red hat thinking was applied to specific ideas. It was not applied to relationships. I did not ask them, 'How do you feel about this team?' or 'How do you feel about Sean?'

(We want to avoid the kind of grenade launched by Georgie that I discussed in chapter 1.)

More significant conversations about the team's emotional intelligence need dedicated time, careful facilitation and, ideally, some pre-assessment.

Emotional conflict typically grows over time, like weeds growing in your garden. But sometimes it flares up suddenly – a bit like the brush turkey that occasionally appears in my garden and leads to me chasing it around until it leaves.

Let's turn to how to manage these emotional flare-ups and unhelpful behaviours.

CALL OUT UNHELPFUL BEHAVIOURS

We're nearing the end of our journey through emotional intelligence. It's time to look at how to deal with unhelpful behaviours in the moment.

The more emotional capital you've built, the less tricky this is. If you've established the foundation and frame that this is a real team, calling out unhelpful behaviours is easier.

If you've co-created behavioural norms, identifying and spotting transgressions is easier.

However, unhelpful behaviours are less common in these situations. Teams who have established a self-identity and behavioural norms are often proficient at keeping conflict focused on the task and not escalating it to relationship conflict.

If unhelpful behaviours consistently occur across the team

In this situation, you need to go back and invest the team's time co-creating the foundations and norms for an Emotionally Intelligent team. Run an assessment to make sure it's not just your perspective, and then take time to reset and form a real team.

If one person consistently crosses the line to unhelpful behaviour

Here, you need to deal directly with that person, helping them see the impact of their behaviours using a combination of feedback and coaching. (For more on team assessment, see the section 'Assess your team's emotional capital', later in this chapter.)

Feedback is useful when the person is not aware of their behaviours. Tell them what you see and what the impact is. Do this with a generous mindset, focused on helping them add more value.

Coaching is useful when they can come up with the solution by thinking it through. Your role is to ask questions that help them work through the facts and the options, and then the plan.

If these changes don't stick, it's time to think about limiting their exposure to the leadership team meetings – and, potentially, taking them out of the core team.

When speaking at re:Work with Google, Anita Williams Woolley outlined that, as part of her research into teams' collective intelligence, she has observed that one negative individual can deplete the overall intelligence of a team. This negativity needs to be the first thing a leader addresses before introducing Woolley's ideas around social perception and conversational turn-taking.

If you see something, say something

At the firm Jackson and Andrews, the leadership team had been working on their annual strategy over an intense two-day offsite.

At 3 pm on day two, the team were finalising the project roadmap and planning how to communicate the strategy to their broader organisation.

Charlie, chief commercial officer, piped up with the following: 'Before we communicate this plan to the organisation, I feel like we all need to buy into it. I don't feel like I've been asked outright if I agree with it.'

Mark, the CEO, responded with, 'We've been working through this for two days. I expect you to voice your concerns without being asked.'

Let's work through this conversation, which lasted just a few seconds.

Charlie's comment was not helpful. It lacked emotional intelligence because it might have triggered other members of the group. However, it could signify some deeper issues. Why has he felt unable to speak up so far? It might not just be his problem.

Mark's reply was direct and immediate. It called out the behaviour and signalled an expected behavioural norm. Mark's tone expressed some annoyance – 'Why raise this now? I thought we were nearly finished. I thought we had buy-in.'

However, for all its clarity and directness, Mark's comment might have made Charlie and others less likely to speak up next time.

What can we learn about calling out unhelpful behaviours?

First of all, if you can, call a break in the meeting and have a quiet word with your Charlie. Don't do it in front of everyone. You may then choose to turn the discussion into a learning for the rest of the team, helping to reinforce behavioural norms.

In my experience, when issues like this need to be raised, I advise people to raise the issue within 24 hours of it happening, but not to raise it when they are annoyed. Wait until you've calmed down.

Publicly signalling the behaviour is not helpful has some benefits, as long as this signalling doesn't cast a negative light on the individual. You could say, for example, 'Charlie, let's have a quick break. You can tell me more, and then we can bring it back to the group if we find it's a helpful topic.'

Second, once you have your Charlie in a one-on-one private conversation, assume there is a good reason, and a positive intent, behind Charlie's comment and ask about it in a neutral way: 'Tell me more about that, Charlie.'

Third, illustrate the impact of Charlie's comment, giving some feedback on how other people might perceive it.

Lastly, check what Charlie has learnt and what he might do differently.

Tactics for dealing with destructive behaviours

Here are some simple tactics to help you deal with the kinds of behaviours that will undermine the team's emotional intelligence:

- *Cabinet responsibility:* A leadership team debates and discusses critical issues. If a team member disagrees with the final decision, they still need to 100 per cent align behind the group's decision when they leave the room. If a team member undermines the team's decisions after the meeting, you'll need to call their behaviour out.
- *The 'no triangles' rule:* This comes from leadership expert Rachael Robertson, who instituted it while leading a team on an Antarctic base. It means 'A doesn't talk to B about C'. For example, Rachel and Rohan don't talk about Sean behind Sean's back. If you have something to say to Sean, step up and say it directly – and constructively. Be helpful.
- *No black hats:* It's useful to voice your concerns and identify risks. It's not useful to *always* be the one person who points out the downside risk. It saps the energy from the room. In de Bono's *Six Hats Thinking*, the black hat (that is, considering risks and negatives) is something the whole team should occasionally wear to collectively surface all the risks. It's not ideal for one person to be the full-time wearer of the black hat.
- *Watch out for the loudest voice and the quietest voice:* As outlined in chapter 4, you need to subtly shift the conversation away from the one or two loudest voices. And, in turn, you need to encourage and reward the quieter people for sharing what they know or asking insightful questions.
- *Call out members who are not listening or not engaging:* You may find a team member showing signs of being disengaged through their body language or comments. And you may find another team member engaged, but not listening to their colleagues' contributions. The disengaged person needs a side conversation to understand and call out their behaviour. The non-listener may benefit from the same kind of one-on-one conversation to identify and address the problem. You can also deal with this non-listener in the moment by asking them to build on or connect to other people's contributions, and to listen to the feedback they're getting.

ASSESS YOUR TEAM'S EMOTIONAL CAPITAL

Comments in annual staff surveys rarely shock me. The following comment, from a survey of the staff of Incisive, a mid-size consulting firm, was the exception, however:

> The appointment of Marie to Director was not dissimilar to Hitler being granted absolute power during the Third Reich. Her removal from the company was a joyous occasion, only trumped by the levelling of the Berlin Wall as one of the great episodes of undoing inhuman injustice in our recent history. The only disappointment was that David Hasselhoff did not sing as she was removed from the premises. Unfortunately, Marie was one of the most dangerous combinations, in that she had considerable confidence and ambition, but was a complete idiot.

Despite the jumps in the modern history of Germany in this comment (from the rise of totalitarian power to the fall of communist rule), the first reading of this comment might lead you to side with the author. Marie must have been awful. But you're only seeing one side. And, whatever the situation with Marie, we don't want people feeling they can only share their feelings by sniping in anonymous surveys. This comment turned out to be the tip of an iceberg-sized team culture problem.

How can you keep a closer eye on the emotional temperature of your team, and not wait for the comments in an annual survey?

Measuring emotional intelligence

In their *Harvard Business Review* article *'Building the emotional intelligence of groups'*, professors Vanessa Druskat and Steven Wolff argue:

> In our study of effective teams, we've found that having norms for group self-awareness – of emotional states, strengths and weaknesses, modes of interaction, and task processes – is a critical part of group emotional intelligence that facilitates group efficacy. Teams gain it both through self-evaluation and by soliciting feedback from others.

So Druskat and Wolff argue that group self-awareness can come from self-evaluation and feedback from others.

No doubt you've tried methods of evaluation and seeking feedback in your organisation. Perhaps you've used the annual staff survey I've already mentioned, or perhaps processes such as seeking 360-degree feedback. But have you measured the awareness and group emotional intelligence of the leadership team?

To measure your team's emotional intelligence, I recommend my Team Intelligence Diagnostic. (Along with measuring the emotional intelligence (EQ) of your leadership team, this tool also measures the team's creative-analytical intelligence (IQ) and practical intelligence (PQ), covered in parts III and IV of this book.) Go to robpyne.online/unlock to access.

The Team Intelligence Diagnostic asks each of your leadership team to assess the team on nine emotionally intelligent behaviours (as well as nine behaviours for IQ and nine for PQ). The diagnostic then outlines the range of scores from your team members, as well as how the average of your scores compares to the benchmarks of many other teams who have taken the survey.

How to act on the assessment results

After gauging the emotional intelligence of your leadership team, you may not need to do anything.

In her article co-authored with Delia Vîrgă, Professor Smaranda Boroş argues that if your team already has good EQ, you may want to avoid spending time discussing further improvements. She has observed teams become swamped in lengthy discussions on emotional intelligence that resulted in little benefit.

Boroş found that if the team comprises individuals with high EQ, creating new group behavioural norms may not add value. However, a team with mixed or low EQ at the individual level can benefit from assessing their collective EQ and putting behavioural norms in place.

The typical result she sees is that groups who can regulate their emotions prevent task conflict turning into relationship conflict. People don't take discussions personally.

If you do need to intervene on your team's emotional intelligence, you may need to take a step back, looking again at building your team's emotional foundations (chapter 3) and layering behavioural norms on top (chapter 4).

Remember – an important part of this process is engaging in dialogue (see chapter 4). Together, the team can discuss the issues and develop solutions.

The foundations

Here's a reminder of the critical principles of emotionally intelligent foundations from chapter 3:

- Redefine why this team exists and what value it creates.
- Make sure it's clear who is in the team.
- Establish the conditions that make this a real team.

The behavioural norms

And here are the fundamental principles for emotionally intelligent behaviours from chapter 4:

- Signals – identify key behaviours (such as vulnerability, turn-taking, intentional relationship-building, whole-person growth) and then signal your recognition when people do them.
- Listening – develop a listening mindset and the skills of active listening.
- Dialogue – create the conditions to add to and build on each other's ideas. Remember that collective thinking beats competitive thinking.

Assessing the team should be regular

Leading a team means being accountable for its ongoing improvement. I recommend measuring your team's EQ (along with its IQ and PQ) every three months and tracking the progress.

In addition to running self-assessments quarterly, I recommend reaching out to the team's stakeholders every six months to get their views on how the leadership team is perceived and the tangible value it has created for them. People who aren't 'in the room where it happens' are unlikely to be able to shed light on the inner workings of the team's emotional intelligence. But their feedback on external perceptions (is this a real team?) and value creation (how are they helping people like you?) can give useful clues and impetus for improving the team's functioning.

TRAPS FOR THE UNWARY

In real life, getting your leadership team together to workshop their emotionally intelligent behaviours is not always straightforward. Don't rush into it. Traps exist here, and I run through some of these in the following sections.

If the team is uncomfortable discussing emotional intelligence

The lower the team's EQ, the more they need to address it. But the lower the team's EQ, the less comfortable they may be talking about it.

One way to encourage a low EQ team to talk is to use the survey results and feedback as a conversation starter – for example, you could use the data from my Team Intelligence Diagnostic in this way. You can make it easier by having the team gather in a semi-circle as you put the assessment results on a screen in front of them. Then you can introduce a conversation about the data and what it means, and elicit contributions from the team to give the data more context. This is a less confrontational way of tackling the issues.

A further risk here is that typical tactics people come up with to introduce behavioural norms often result in new processes – for example, introducing a rule of always having an agenda for meetings as a way of stopping the meeting being dominated by one or two people. If this tendency towards processes starts appearing, you may want to run through some evidence for what is proven to increase team EQ and ask all members to build on those ideas. The areas to focus on are discussed in much more detail in chapter 4, but a hint for now: having agendas for your leadership team meetings is unlikely to improve the team's EQ.

If the team's emotional conflict issues centre on one person

Having one member of the leadership team who drags down the whole team's energy and productivity is not uncommon – perhaps Marie, mentioned earlier in this chapter, was this person in her leadership team (and ended up being likened to a certain German dictator).

If you have a Marie in your team, having all-hands discussions and selecting new behavioural norms is probably not the solution. Instead try one-on-one coaching from the leader, helping the person gain awareness of the impact of their behaviours. If that fails, it may be time to move them out of the leadership team's inner circle. They can still contribute, stay informed and make guest appearances, but they don't need to be at every meeting. Likely, they don't enjoy these meetings anyway. So as long as you can manage their ego, it may be better for everyone if they aren't in the team.

If the team's emotional conflict issues centre on one person and that person is you (or your leader)

Earlier, we looked at the story of Rachel and her leader Brian. Brian's heart was in the right place, but his EQ skills didn't rise to the level of acknowledging Rachel's vulnerability.

It is not unheard of, in my experience, for the leader of the team to be the one creating emotional conflict.

If you have an inkling that your own EQ needs some work, you would be wise to get some feedback from your team – and then thank them for it, and develop some new approaches. These new approaches could include aspects outlined in chapter 4, such as signalling recognition, listening more and bringing out the voices of the quieter people.

Unfortunately, sometimes the leaders with the lowest EQ are the least aware of the problem.

If you are reading this as a leadership team member whose leader has a low EQ, *Multipliers*, by Liz Wiseman (with Greg McKeown), provides some insights. In this book, Wiseman contrasts people who are *multipliers* with those who are *diminishers*. Multipliers bring out the best in others, while diminishers reduce others' impact.

Wiseman breaks down her advice if your boss is a diminisher into two levels of strategy.

Level 1 strategies focus on building your defences, including:

- turning down the volume – choose your reaction to their behaviours
- strengthening your connections with other teammates
- retreating and regrouping – take time to think, don't react in the moment
- sending the right signals – show that you also value what they value.

Level 2 strategies are about bringing out the best in your boss through the following:

- acknowledging and exploiting their strengths
- telling them what you're good at and how to get the best out of you
- listening to learn – choose what you can learn from their critiques of you
- admitting your mistakes and owning the solutions.

Chapter summary

As a member (or leader) of your leadership team, you need to pay regular attention to the team's emotional intelligence. You need to consciously signal your support for positive behaviours and call out unhelpful behaviours.

Over time, as the team builds its own behavioural norms, your focus on emotional intelligence will become less critical, and the team will manage itself more easily. That's the benefit of building the foundations and setting the behavioural norms.

Take action

Actively manage the emotions of the team through:

- Checking ins at the start of meetings to provide multiple benefits in building a real team that supports its members.
- Surfacing emotional reactions to ideas by asking people to share their immediate gut feel about the content.
- Calling out unhelpful behaviours promptly without making the individual feel bad.
- Undertaking quarterly assessments based on surveys of the leadership team, using tools such as my Team Intelligence Diagnostic (see robpyne.online/unlock).

Next

Now that you've addressed your team's emotional intelligence, you have the foundations to unlock their collective IQ and apply it to your most challenging problems and most important strategies. The chapters in the following part explore creative-analytical intelligence.

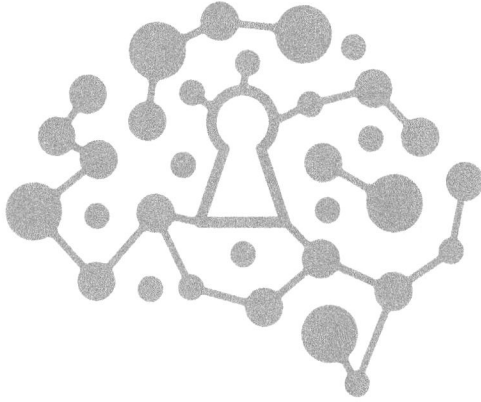

PART III

UNLOCKING THE TEAM'S CREATIVE-ANALYTICAL INTELLIGENCE

INTRODUCING THREE-DIMENSIONAL PROBLEM-SOLVING AND TEAM IQ

We were one hour into a leadership team discussion on marketing. The debate was locked into whether we should have a YouTube channel, Twitter account, or LinkedIn page for our business. Then someone asked, 'What exactly is the problem we're trying to solve?'

We all looked at each other. Oops. We were carried away discussing answers, without knowing the question. We had wasted an hour of discussion on the merits of LinkedIn versus Twitter.

Once we'd been brought back down to earth, we were able to define the underlying question: 'How can we generate more new business leads among clients we haven't met?'

This problem has a wider range of solutions than Twitter, LinkedIn and YouTube. Other options could include PR, events, white papers – even writing a book.

This story, from a leadership team I worked in, illustrates some of the challenges of bringing a group of smart individuals together to solve problems.

I like to think of problems as having three dimensions, and the challenges for leadership teams often stem from not addressing all three dimensions. First, let me outline these three dimensions of problems:

- They have a *depth*, which requires you to get under the surface to understand what the real issue is.
- They have a *width*, which means you need to consider a wide range of potential solutions.
- And they have a *length*, and this time span, heading into the future, asks you to think further ahead than this week or this quarter.

That means the creative and analytical thinking required to solve problems is quite expansive. And yet leadership teams don't always think expansively: their thinking can be shallow, narrow and short term.

> ....
> **Often, we don't identify the real problem. I call this *shallow thinking*. We come up with a small range of options. I call this *narrow thinking*. And we tend to think only about this week or this quarter. I call this *short-term thinking*.**
> ....

To counteract these tendencies, in the chapters in this part, I investigate three ways to stretch your team's creative and analytical intelligence – their collective IQ.

In chapter 6, we go deeper and explore how to think more deeply about the root causes of problems.

In chapter 7, we go wider to help your team generate more options.

In chapter 8, we go further to help you think further ahead and longer term.

Without doubt, today's leadership teams need to be highly skilled at strategic thinking, critical thinking, analytical thinking and creative problem-solving.

As already highlighted through this book, an increasing research effort from the MIT Centre for Collective Intelligence – and others – reveals that teams have a mind of their own. A team's intelligence depends more on the team's dynamics than on the intelligence of individual team members.

Creating an environment where your team can collectively go deeper, think wider, and plan further ahead allows you to unlock your team's true potential.

6

Deeper.
Thinking deeper to crack problems.

SEARCHING FOR THE LOST BALL

A strange thing happens to golfers when they lose a ball in the long grass. To search for it, they adopt a strategy I call the 'random walk'. Instead of organising themselves and combing the area in straight lines, they stay close together and make rough circles and zig-zags like a fly making loops and laps in your kitchen.

This random walk is also how many leadership teams attempt to work through unfamiliar terrain and find answers.

When groups of people discuss a problem, they fall prey to specific errors, as behavioural psychologists Cass Sunstein and Reid Hastie show in their book *Wiser: Getting Beyond Groupthink to Make Groups Smarter*.

They spend too much time circling one part of the puzzle.

They stay in the 'shorter grass', or the areas that are more familiar and comfortable.

They cluster together around the loudest people.

In short, their approach is a higgledy-piggledy random walk.

In this chapter, I explore how your team can work through a problem to understand the issues more deeply and ensure a shared understanding of cause and effect. In other words, I help your team navigate through the 'long grass' and find the ball.

I call this going deeper, and so I also explore three ways to unlock the intelligence you need to go deeper:

1. looking at the situation from different perspectives
2. shining the light on what you don't know
3. considering how all the parts of the system affect each other.

These approaches sound straightforward, but it's surprising how rarely leadership teams deploy them. Instead, they stay in the short grass.

LOOKING AT THE SITUATION FROM DIFFERENT PERSPECTIVES

In *Which Two Heads Are Better than One?*, Deloitte executive Juliet Bourke identifies six different perspectives leadership team members can take on an issue. These are focused on:

- Options – what can we do?
- Outcomes – what does success look like?
- Risk – what might go wrong?
- People – how might this affect our people?
- Process – are we following the process?
- Evidence – do we have enough data and evidence?

Bourke also demonstrated that 75 per cent of senior leaders spend too much time on options or outcomes – the two areas many feel are most useful for making decisions.

She called this 'too much time' because research showed that when teams went through all six perspectives – not just options and outcomes – they made more effective decisions. Bourke notes:

> University of Michigan Professors Hong and Page calculated a 30 per cent error rate when problems are solved via the application of one dominant approach – and conversely a 100 per cent accuracy rate when five different approaches are applied.

Integrating these different perspectives is one of the fundamental reasons to put problems in front of teams. The team can listen and build on the different perspectives to create a deeper understanding of a problem.

However, team leaders don't always facilitate this well, often paying too much attention to the loud and powerful voices.

Google's extensive research into what makes teams effective, codenamed Project Aristotle, found 'psychological safety' was a significant predictor of team results. Within this, they found good teams had equality of conversational turn-taking, and not-so-good teams had unequal turn-taking, with certain people taking most of the airtime. (For more on working with loud and quiet people, refer to chapter 4.)

The team leader speaking first will also generally reduce the diversity of perspectives, because people tend to fall in line with the 'hippo' – the highest-paid person's opinion.

To quote Wharton professor Adam Grant,

> The most dangerous voice in a meeting is the HIPPO: The Highest Paid Person's Opinion. Status disparities can fuel conformity and groupthink. When you need diversity of thought, ask everyone else to share their views before turning to the HIPPO.

If the discussion isn't structured with different perspectives considered, it will go round in circles or leap around between disconnected issues.

....
**If the loud people are left unchecked,
the quietest people's perspectives will go unheard.**
....

Two approaches to broaden your perspective

The following sections outline two approaches to look at problems from multiple perspectives. Both create a deeper understanding of a problem.

Equal airtime

The first approach is to take advantage of the naturally diverse perspectives in the room. As I like to say, 'Everyone has a piece of the puzzle,' so you should create the environment where everyone can share their perspective, and then you can put all these pieces together and see the bigger picture.

Further evidence for the benefits of equality of airtime comes from the MIT Centre for Collective Intelligence. As researchers from MIT (and other universities) outline in 'Evidence for a collective intelligence factor in the performance of human groups', a significant predictor of a team's problem-solving ability is 'the equality of conversational turn-taking'.

Simply put, groups in the study were less effective at solving a range of complex problems when a small number of voices dominated their discussion.

And yet it sounds tiresome to let each team member provide input into every issue facing the leadership team. Shouldn't we give more airtime as required to subject matter experts?

The answer is yes. But that is different from allowing the loud people to dominate.

To build a range of perspectives and equality of airtime, follow this three-step approach:

1. Gather perspectives from the subject matter experts in your team (and, if necessary, invite in other subject matter experts from your organisation).
2. Ask the other group members to contribute additional perspectives (even contradictory ones) or ask clarifying questions.
3. Ensure the leader speaks last to add their perspective. I call this the 'leader speaks last' rule. It's a good challenge for the many leaders who are passionate about their business and whose natural tendency is to suggest solutions quickly. If you're the leader, remember that speaking first will not serve the overall success of the team. (Unless your ideas *are* always the best, of course!)

Perspective tours

The second approach allows you to move beyond the naturally occurring diversity in the room, and involves encouraging the whole team to shift through a range of perspectives simultaneously – a bit like going on a tour together.

You can even choose between different tours.

The first could be based on Bourke's six perspectives (outlined earlier in this chapter). In this case, you could make sure the group moves through multiple perspectives such as evidence, risk, people and process – as well as the more common outcomes and options.

The secret to any perspective 'tour' is to stay together as a group. Having everyone discuss the evidence at once is more useful than one person talking about the process, and another talking about the evidence.

The most famous version of the perspective tour is Edward de Bono's *Six Hat Thinking*. De Bono's breakthrough idea was to name six styles of thinking, and then encourage teams to work through them one at a time. He called this 'parallel thinking', and it's a forerunner to Bourke's six perspectives. The six hats are a little more attitudinal (about how you think) and a little less functional (what you think about).

Here's my summary of the hats:

- The white hat focuses on the facts.
- The red hat asks about your gut feel.
- The yellow hat looks at the positives of an idea.
- The black hat considers the risks and negatives.
- The green hat opens up new possibilities – what if, what else?
- The blue hat guides the process – which hat shall we use next? How much time do we have left?

In a real-life case outlined by de Bono in *Six Thinking Hats*, Statoil in Norway had a problem with an oil rig that was costing $100,000 a day. By applying the six hats method, they solved the problem in 12 minutes.

Practical application of perspective-taking

You've seen the evidence that diversity of perspective can lead to better outcomes. I have also alluded to the idea that it is quicker, which might appear counterintuitive.

While it may sound convoluted to ask everyone's opinion or go on a perspective tour, it can actually be quicker, as it was in de Bono's Statoil case study. That's because when groups engage in unstructured discussions about issues, they tend to go on many low-value tangents and spend too much time on the areas people already know well and agree on.

....

A structured approach to perspective-taking means each contribution in the conversation adds value, and you can curtail the tangents that torture many leadership teams.

....

Again in *Six Thinking Hats*, de Bono showed that his technique can reduce meeting duration by up to 75 per cent – for example, from 4 hours to 45 minutes in one instance for an Optus management team in Australia.

And research conducted by Erik Larson, founder of decision-making collaboration software Cloverpop, showed that teams that follow an inclusive process make decisions twice as quickly with half the number of meetings.

When you don't want more perspectives

At times when you're leading a meeting you will realise more perspectives are not needed. Typically, this might happen when you have a large leadership team – say, 11 people or more – and you are discussing a low-value issue.

In this instance, you can flip the focus and ask for questions instead of opinions. Instead of asking for the next person's opinion, flip to, 'What questions do the rest of the group have to clarify the situation before we make a decision?'

If people are not experts in the subject at hand – for example, the HR leader is commenting on the CFO's area or vice versa – you can leverage their respective brainpower by encouraging them to use smart questions that help the subject matter experts consider different perspectives.

Here are some example questions:

- *Big picture questions:* How does this connect to our business strategy? Who needs to make this decision?
- *Detail questions:* What other evidence could help us decide? When do we need to decide by?
- *Future questions:* What does success look like? What might the consequences be?
- *Past questions:* What can we learn from the past? Have we done anything similar before?

Don't be golfers, be detectives

If you take a structured approach to understanding the situation, your leadership team will act less like a bunch of amateur golfers searching for a lost ball.

In fact, you might end up feeling more like a group of professional police searchers combing the long grass for a clue, working together systematically to cover critical areas one at a time. And you'll be much more likely to create a shared understanding, be closer to the truth and nearer to finding an answer.

SHINING THE LIGHT ON WHAT YOU DON'T KNOW

The idea of gathering all the perspectives of the team is built on two assumptions. First, the assumption of diverse expertise: the idea that gathering the different aspects of what everyone knows is useful. Second, the assumption of diverse experience: that people's life experience lends them different ways of exploring a problem.

In a business world built on innovation, we can't always rely on experience and expertise to solve problems. Often unknowns will pop up that are beyond the team's existing knowledge.

It turns out these unknowns can be your friend – they can even be a source of competitive advantage. This comes through turning known unknowns to known knowns, and by turning unknown unknowns to known unknowns.

Unknown unknowns

become

Known unknowns

become

Known knowns

(With a hat-tip to Donald Rumsfeld.)

Acknowledging the unknowns in a business situation can lead to better decisions. In 'The case for behavioural strategy' Dan Lovallo and Oliver Sibony tracked 1048 real-life business decisions. They found the 'explicit exploration of major uncertainties [and] inclusion of perspectives that contradict the senior leader's point of view' were significant predictors of the long-term outcome of decisions.

....

**Discussing what you don't know
helps teams make better decisions.**

....

Looking into the negative space

To deal with what you don't know, you first need to acknowledge your knowledge gaps – something that is sometimes easier said than done. It's not that leadership teams think they are omniscient. It's just they tend to gloss over the gaps and ignore the holes.

A useful metaphor is the artistic concept of negative space. Imagine a picture of a tree's branches. The shapes of each branch, from the outline inwards, are the positive space. Our attention is drawn to the positive space. The area between and around the branches is the negative space. And it's quite hard to notice the negative space if you're looking at the branches.

Negative spaces are the gaps between things. They are the unknown unknowns, the unspoken wisdom in a meeting, the periphery of our view.

Evidence is increasingly highlighting that paying attention to the edges – the opposites, the negative space – is good for business.

The positives of negative space

One example of this evidence first looks at the way humans tend to focus on confirming what we want to be true. This is known as 'confirmation bias'.

People who believe vaccines are dangerous, for example, will interpret any new information about vaccines as support for their pre-existing view, or discount the information altogether. This is a robust, well-replicated finding.

And confirmation bias is one reason leadership teams tend to gravitate towards a comfortable, familiar – and shallow – understanding of a situation.

....

To go deeper, shine your light into the negative space. That's where you can move beyond the common knowledge and find uncommon wisdom – a deeper understanding of your consumer or competitor, clearer priorities, and unforeseen risks.

....

Turning unknown unknowns into known knowns

If you have already listened to your team's perspectives on an issue and taken a perspective tour, you have already created a good map of the 'problem space' – the areas of your business relevant to this discussion.

To look into the gaps in your map, you need to ask a specific series of questions. (You have probably noticed that sometimes the smartest people don't have all the answers, but they often ask the best questions.)

To make sure you create a deeper understanding of the problem – or an even better map of the problem space – I recommend moving in four directions to stretch your perspective. Think of stretching in these four directions as being similar to the moves available using a joystick:

1. First, think bigger by moving the joystick UP. Ask questions that get you and your team thinking up in the bigger picture, such as why you're doing this and whether it fits with your overall strategy.
2. Second, explore the detail by moving the joystick DOWN. Ask questions that dig down into the details of when, how, what and how much?
3. Third, dig into the past by moving the joystick LEFT. Ask questions that call on previous projects and previous knowledge.
4. Fourth, head into a future perspective by moving the joystick RIGHT. Ask questions that play out the consequences and imagine future success and failure.

This joystick model, and the kinds of questions to be asking when stretching in each direction, is shown in figure 6.1.

Figure 6.1: The joystick model of questioning

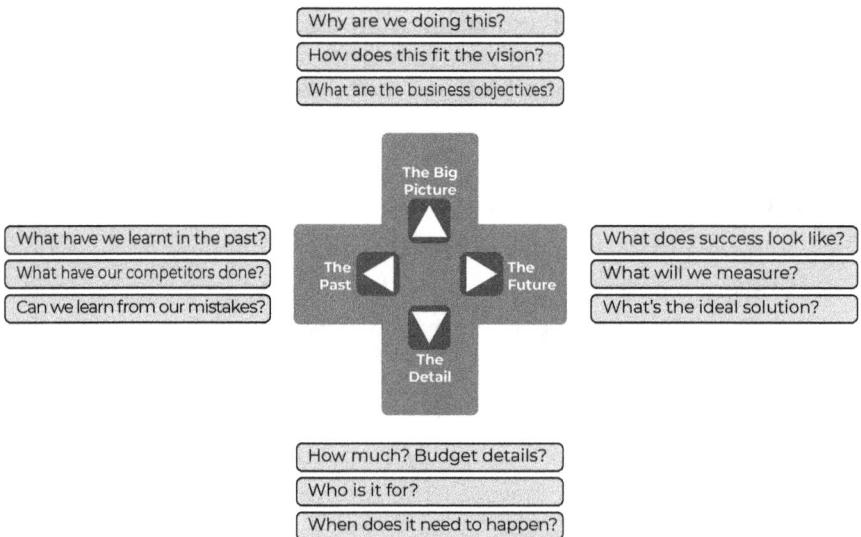

Note that these are the same four types of questions I discussed earlier in this chapter, in the section 'When you don't want more perspectives', which help you get the best out of people who are not experts in the topic-at-hand.

You can use these non-subject matter experts to ask great questions that stretch the perspective of the experts in the room and help the group explore the negative space.

....

Good questioning is the art of organising our thinking around what we don't know. Good questioning is a mark of an intelligent team.

....

Being wrong is good

It's almost a cliché to praise the importance of failure these days. 'Fail fast,' they say. If you're not failing, you're not trying hard enough.

It's also vital for leaders and leadership teams to not just get things wrong, but also to admit to *being wrong*.

In *Being Wrong*, Kathryn Schulz explores our human attachment to being right:

> We all know everybody in this room makes mistakes. The human species, in general, is fallible – okay, fine. But when it comes down to me, right now, to all the beliefs I hold, here in the present tense, suddenly all of this abstract appreciation of fallibility goes out the window – and I can't actually think of anything I'm wrong about.

Other research outlined in 'How leader humility helps teams to be humbler, psychologically stronger, and more effective' highlights that leadership teams benefit from the intellectual humility of considering their beliefs might be wrong, right now.

In *The Fifth Discipline*, Peter Senge emphasises the difference between discussion and dialogue.

Discussion is where opposing views are surfaced and debated. Linking in with the discussion of debate versus dialogue I outline in chapter 4, this kind of discussion involves competitive thinking, where robust debate ends up in a winning and losing argument. It is a zero-sum game, with the focus on being right and winning – not learning.

On the other hand, dialogue is where each team member contributes their knowledge, and the team searches out a deeper understanding of the situation. The focus is on collective learning, not on individually being right.

Exploring the unknowns

In one of the first team decision-making workshops I ever ran, the team in question had a key client who had given them a client review score of 6 out of 10, which was deemed a problem. The team had begun to discuss why this had happened and what to do.

'Tell me about the 6 out of 10,' I said. 'How do you know that?'

'We sent a survey, and 6 was the average score.'

'How many on the client team answered the survey?'

'Five people.'

'How many people are in the client team?'

'The team has 23 members.'

'So only five out of 23 completed the survey. And did the most senior clients fill in the survey?'

'No, only some of the less senior ones.'

As a result of this short discussion, the focus of the team dialogue changed to one of exploring the unknowns. How could they understand how the whole client team felt, especially the more senior ones?

This story illustrates the need to identify the quality of your knowledge, and the opportunity to explicitly separate the facts from the assumptions from the unknowns.

It reveals the opportunity to go deeper and ask questions about the unknowns – to again shine your light into the negative space.

To get to right, you have to go through wrong

We humans spend far too much time and effort defending and reinforcing our positions and our ideas.

One of the benefits of having a leadership team should be to help you shine a light on what you don't know and help you work out where you're getting things wrong.

....

By developing an environment of intellectual humility, curiosity and exploration – perspective stretching, even – your team will deepen their understanding of your business.

....

The temptation to stick with what you know

You might be concerned that the exploration of unknowns can be long-winded and fruitless. Or you may worry that being wrong will feel bad. Isn't it better to stick with what you know?

If I were a leader 50 years ago, I might have agreed. Back then, if you found a good business model, you could develop strategies with five-year horizons. Business was incremental. Change was slow. Competition wasn't global.

These days, one of the significant components of long-term survival is not 'What's your strategy for the next five years?', but 'How can you speed up how quickly your organisation learns?'

Two great ways of increasing your speed of learning are to explore unknowns and to question your assumptions.

CONSIDERING HOW ALL THE PARTS AFFECT EACH OTHER

Why did Donald Trump beat Hillary Clinton in the 2016 US presidential election? You can find plenty of articles that attempt to find the cause that explains the effect.

Some of them point at a singular cause – for example, FBI Director James Comey's announcement in the week before election day that they were investigating Hillary's emails. Others look deeper, trying to work out how a number of underlying causes came together.

If you look over most news articles on any given day, you'll generally be looking at an article trying to describe a news event and identify a singular cause.

We humans are cause-and-effect-analysis machines. But we have some flaws in our software.

We focus on the specific details in the system (how the James Comey announcement affected the election outcome, or the effect of Clinton calling Trump supporters 'deplorables'), and we neglect the relationships between them (how the people offended by Clinton then reacted to the Comey announcement).

Thinking about the interactions and relationships between parts of the system is called, rather unimaginatively, 'systems thinking'.

A proper investigation of systems thinking is beyond the scope of this book. However, you can use practical tools to gain a deeper understanding of the system (that is, market sector) you're in and how its different parts affect each other.

The following sections outline some of these tools and models.

The Business Model Canvas

In 2005, business theorist and entrepreneur Alex Osterwalder embarked on a challenge – to find the best way to represent a business model.

In the past, people had created business plans, but these were often long documents detailing everything about a business and its future direction.

Osterwalder's innovation, along with several hundred collaborators, was to create a way to describe any organisation's business model using nine building blocks and then arrange those building blocks onto a one-page diagram where the relationships between them became apparent. In doing so, Osterwalder had visually represented the business as a system.

Osterwalder calls this the Business Model Canvas, shown in figure 6.2.

The Business Model Canvas helps business owners and strategists – and leadership teams – to think about their business using a simplified version of the systems-thinking approach:

- If I change my ideal customer (top-right of the model), do I also need to change the value proposition (middle) and cost structure (bottom-left)?

Figure 6.2: The Business Model Canvas

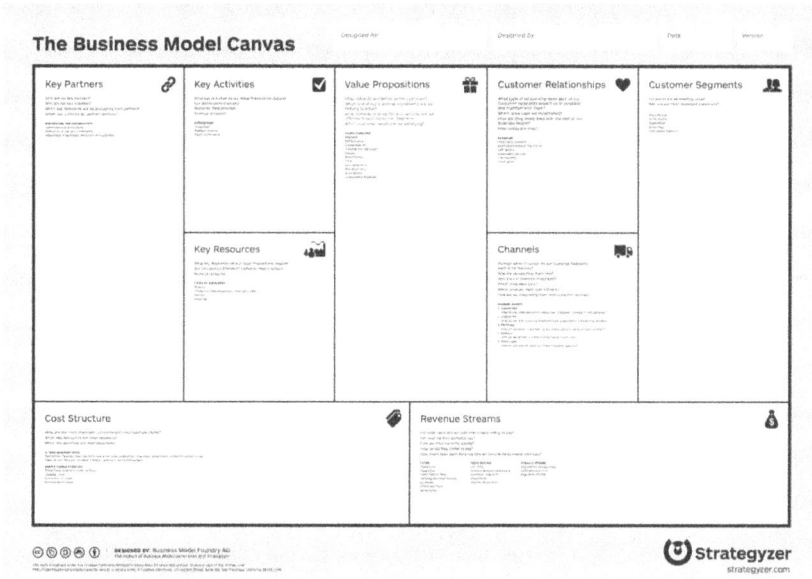

Source: Alex Osterwalder, Businessmodelalchemist.com/tools. Reproduced under a Creative Commons Attribution Share-Alike 1.0 Generic license.

- Are my key activities (left) consistent with my ideal customers, or with my value proposition?

In other words, the team can now consider the impact of a change to one of the nine blocks on the other eight.

The nine blocks in the Business Model Canvas can also be used to help you generate a business dashboard – for example, through picking the key result areas from among the nine boxes. (For more on goal setting and dashboards, see chapter 9.)

Building your own mental models

Creating a deeper understanding of a situation, a problem or a whole business rarely means finding the absolute truth of how everything works. Instead, it means making a better mental model.

The Business Model Canvas is, as its name suggests, a tool to help you build a mental model of your whole business, not just its separate functions.

It sounds frivolous until you realise many leadership team members don't have a working mental model of their whole business. And that means they may be contributing to whole-of-business decisions while only considering a narrow slice of the issue.

In the following sections, I look at this limitation, and discuss creating shared mental models with your leadership team.

Incomplete mental models

Working with a senior and experienced leadership team, I facilitated a strategy development process over a series of workshops. In workshop one, we looked at product-market fit – what were their buyers' needs and how well did their current products deliver? Around half of the team did not have a solid understanding of the company's product mix. The Group CEO decided to add a series of educational sessions for the leadership team to get up to speed.

Visible, shared mental models

Mike Maples is a venture capitalist at Floodgate Venture Capital. Maples makes money by assessing companies for investment potential. During an interview with Shane Parrish, Mike discussed how his competitive advantage comes from developing better shared mental models on what makes a good company to invest in.

His team has taken to writing down and refining these mental models over time. They use them as a series of rules – for example:

> Most of the great start-ups come from a great insight, and a great insight usually occurs when someone is living in the future, and they notice something that's missing.

The most important mental models

This book is full of mental models I have created or borrowed to help people better understand the systems they work in. Among the most useful in my experience are the:

- the joystick model of questions (see earlier in this chapter)
- visible project roadmap (see chapter 9)

- strategic business dashboard (see chapter 10)
- strategy house (see chapter 13).

Each of these models is designed to create shared understanding of what's important and how things affect each other. Where they add even more value is when they go beyond the leadership team and become known by the wider team. For example:

- A successful leader of a $250-million business makes sure everyone in the organisation knows the business vision and top four goals this quarter.
- Another leadership team creates a strategy house and launches it at a two-day all-staff offsite to make sure everyone understands where they fit and what they need to do.
- A leadership team in a non-profit uses a version of the Business Model Canvas to check whether their business model is viable and receive input from the wider team.

Whenever you're dealing with a complex problem, finding a model that helps explain it is always helpful.

Another option is to create one yourself by outlining the dimensions of the problem using one of three classic models: a quadrant chart, pyramid or Venn diagram. (Examples of these are shown in figure 6.3.)

Figure 6.3: Three basic models that can help you understand a problem, and share your understanding with others

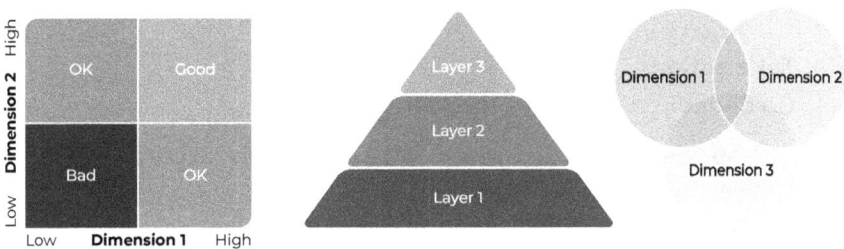

REPEATING THE PROCESS

This chapter focuses on going deeper to understand cause and effect better. But it's important to remember the process is not only about going deeper once.

Let's say you've had a good leadership team meeting where you discussed an issue, gathered everyone's perspective and developed more insight.

Now you need to consolidate this new level of depth, and you need to make sure it's shared, make sure it's visible, and make sure you continue to gain an even deeper understanding moving forward.

Chapter summary

As a leadership team, you need to go deeper into problems to understand the causes and effects more fully. This involves looking at issues from multiple perspectives, and trying to turn unknown unknowns into known knowns.

It also involves getting comfortable with being wrong, and using mental models to develop a better understanding of how different parts of your business work together as a system.

Importantly, any insights that come through these discussions and processes need to be communicated with everyone in the business.

Take action

Go deeper on problems through the following:

- Use your team's diverse experience and expertise to unlock a deeper understanding of a situation. Take a perspective tour.
- Shine the light on the unknowns by asking better questions. Use the joystick framework to pick from four types of questions.

- Consider a problem as a system of interconnected parts by drawing a mental model of the elements and considering how they affect each other. The Business Model Canvas is one model you can use to understand your business, set goals, and look at how strategies may play out.

Next

Once you've gained a deeper understanding of a problem, it's time to consider how to solve it by widening your team's thinking – the topic of the next chapter.

7

Wider.
Thinking wider to unlock your team's best ideas.

FIGHTING FIRES

A fire engine comes screeching to a halt outside a burning house. The fire-fighters leap out. Where's the fire coming from? How bad is it? Are there people in there? How will they fight it?

Gary Klein is a research psychologist specialising in naturalistic – that is, real-world – decision-making. He has interviewed and observed many fire teams in action. How do they answer these questions, and how do they make decisions?

Here's what they don't do:

- They don't call a meeting.
- They don't have a long discussion about the situation.
- They don't consider everyone's opinion.
- And they definitely don't make a spreadsheet comparing the benefits of different approaches.

Instead, Klein's observations of fire-fighters in action revealed a pattern he called 'recognition-primed decision-making'. Here's how it works.

The most experienced fire-fighter is in charge.

When they look at the fire, they subconsciously compare it to all the previous fires they've attended it. (This is the 'recognition' piece of the process.)

They surface one potential solution based on their previous experiences. (They are 'primed' with an initial idea.)

They mentally 'play forward' what might happen if they apply that solution. (Okay, so it looks like the fire is coming from the basement, it's already spread to the ground floor, which means we need to go in via ladders to the top floor ... let's play that out, does it feel like it will work here?)

If it seems like the solution will work when they play it forward, they go with it. There's no time to waste comparing multiple options.

They get immediate feedback on whether their plan worked or not, so they can calibrate their decisions. In situation A, they know that action B reliably works.

This system generally works for fire-fighters. Why?

- It's based on their experience – recognising the patterns from fires they've seen in the past.
- It's quick, with most of the mental work happening subconsciously. That requires less conscious effort.
- It provides fast and clear feedback on whether the plan worked, so decision-making becomes more reliable over time.

The process has limitations, as well. It fails when the nature of the fire in front of you has been misdiagnosed – the fire has already reached the top floor, perhaps, without them realising.

And it fails when the fire is unusual, and the lead fire-fighter doesn't have the relevant experience to draw on – the house in question is a new type of eco-friendly carbon-fibre-framed house, perhaps, which they don't have any experience with.

Assuming you are not a senior team leader fighting actual fires, how is this relevant to you?

Evidence suggests that, in business, we often make decisions like these fire-fighters. We generate one option. Often it comes from the leader. The option is based on previous experience. We play out the option to see if it will work. If it does, we stop thinking and go with it.

If you're making urgent life-and-death decisions in your business, I recommend you get good at recognition-primed decision-making. You can do this by increasing your bank of experience, and making sure you learn what works and what doesn't from your previous decisions.

But perhaps your decisions aren't life and death?

Perhaps you have at least a few hours to think it through?

Perhaps it's not 100 per cent clear if your previous decisions were right?

Perhaps you're dealing with novel situations no-one has seen before?

In these cases, you will be better to draw breath, widen your focus, and generate more options – and that's what this chapter is all about. To help you take this breath and widen your focus, I look at different ways of thinking – such as divergent and diamond-shaped thinking – before converging on a solution.

HAVING MORE THAN ONE OPTION: FIGHTING FIRES VERSUS STARTING FIRES

The decisions and problems you face with your leadership team can be broadly divided into two types: fire-fighting and fire-starting:

- *Fire-fighting decisions:* These are made when you want to solve a problem quickly. It's reactive, and based on experience. You and the team generate a good-enough option and then move on.
- *Fire-starting decisions:* These are made when you are trying to start something. You see a potential opportunity – perhaps a gap in the market. It's a novel situation. You generate several options and compare them, and then you try one approach. You can always change tack.

In leadership teams, it is useful to frame discussions and decisions around these differences. Is this a fire-fighting situation, or a fire-starting situation?

Do you want a quick, good-enough fix to a small issue?

Or do you want to run an extensive search for a way forward?

The benefits of extra options

Professor Paul Nutt, author of *Why Decisions Fail*, investigated 168 real business decisions. In 71 per cent of these cases, the organisations only had one new alternative on the table. The following are examples of a choice between the status quo and one new alternative:

· Should we launch this product?
· Should we acquire this business?
· Should we enter this new market?

Nutt went on to track long-term outcomes of these decisions. When organisations had only one new alternative, their choice failed 52 per cent of the time. When they generated at least two new alternatives, the failure rate reduced to 32 per cent.

Examples of decisions with two new alternatives include the following:

· Should we launch this new product, or invest the money in improving our existing product?
· Should we acquire this business, or run a share buyback?
· Should we enter this new market, or add a new distribution partner in a current market?

Having one extra option creates a substantial impact. The likelihood of your long-term success rises from 48 per cent (less than even) to 68 per cent (more than two-thirds right).

Avoiding analysis paralysis

Whether you are fire-fighting or fire-starting, you may perceive a risk here. Perhaps generating more options will slow your decision-making down, or even lead to analysis paralysis?

You can avoid these risks if your problem is clearly defined. Decisions can slow down when the multiple options reflect an underlying challenge: that the exact nature of the problem is not clear to everyone. Then the solutions that get put on the table are solving different problems – which means it's hard to compare them. And it means it may feel too early to decide because you need to go back a step and define the problem more clearly.

If the problem itself is clear, evidence suggests having multiple options leads to a *quicker* decision. That's because we can gain confidence from picking the best from a series of options – compared to being uncertain if we only have one option.

In 'Strategic decision-making in high-velocity environments', researchers Kevin Clark and Christopher Collins found that simultaneously assessing multiple options was one way to speed up decisions – along with having real-time data on business performance and linking individual decisions to the broader strategy.

And in *Decisive*, brothers Chip and Dan Heath specifically consider whether having multiple options leads to analysis paralysis. After reviewing all available literature, they argue, 'The best evidence … is that decision paralysis is not likely to occur until the number of options moves past six'.

....

Having more options reduces the risk of failure and helps teams make decisions faster.

....

How should leadership teams generate more options? Divergent thinking is one place to start.

USING DIVERGENT THINKING TO UNLOCK YOUR TEAM'S BEST IDEAS

Groups use two basic styles of thinking:

- *Convergent thinking:* When a group is employing convergent thinking, they are trying to reach an agreement. They are making a decision, choosing an option, prioritising, aligning and agreeing. This is a process of narrowing and reaching consensus.
- *Divergent thinking:* In this mode, the team is exploring, trying to find different options. They are brainstorming, coming up with options and thinking out of the box. This is a process of widening the view, broadening the discussion.

The inherent conflict between convergent and divergent thinking

In Sam Kaner's excellent book *The Facilitator's Guide to Participatory Decision-Making*, he highlights a conflict within convergent and divergent thinking styles.

Let's say you're half an hour into a discussion. You're trying to decide whether to enter a new market now, or wait. At this point in the meeting, some of the team are ready to make a decision. They feel that enough facts and options have been tabled; it's time to make a call and move on. Time to converge.

Simultaneously, some of the team have only just got going. They don't think any of the existing discussion or options have illuminated the way forward. They want the thinking to keep diverging.

Kaner refers to this as the 'groan zone' where people start to get frustrated. Half the team think you're moving too slowly and going round in circles, while the other half think it's going too quickly.

USING DIAMOND-SHAPED THINKING INSTEAD

The solution to this inherent conflict between convergent and divergent thinking is to employ what I call *diamond-shaped thinking* to run your discussions. The way this combines convergent and divergent thinking is shown in figure 7.1.

Let's say you have an hour to discuss the timing of market entry. You start by clearly laying out the problem. Then you explicitly allocate half the meeting to divergent thinking. Let's explore, ask everyone's perspective, and develop at least two to three viable options. That takes you to half past the hour.

At that point, you shift to convergent thinking (avoiding the groan zone) and move to make a decision. This provides a sense of the best two options and allows everyone time to compare them. By the end of the hour, you should try to reach a consensus decision. If that is not possible, the leader or critical decision-maker makes a call – or defers a decision to gather more information.

Figure 7.1: Diamond-shaped thinking

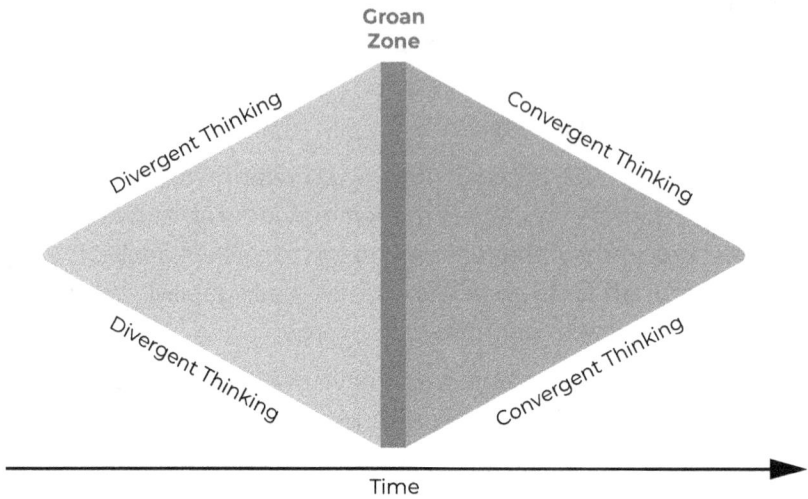

The keys to diamond-shaped thinking are:

· Have a clear problem definition at the start of the meeting.
· Allocate specific time constraints for divergent and convergent thinking.
· Actively manage the conversation – otherwise, you'll find people wanting to add new ideas at the last minute, or people wanting to make a decision or rule out an option before you reach halfway.
· Define the rules for how you'll make a final decision.

CREATE DIVERGENT OPTIONS

At the heart of divergent thinking are two ideas.

First, you use the team's cognitive diversity. Their experience and expertise and styles should naturally surface different potential solutions. The team can then build on these diverse options. As Alison Reynolds and David Lewis showed in their *Harvard Business Review* article, teams solve problems more quickly when they're more cognitively diverse.

To leverage cognitive diversity, you merely need to hold the group in the divergent thinking space and ask for more options. Canvass each person's perspective. If you have created the right emotionally intelligent foundations and behaviours (refer to the chapters in part II), ideas should flow. You'll get more options, and you'll get the immediate uplift which Professor Nutt described: as soon as you have a second viable option, your chance of long-term success increases from 48 per cent to 68 per cent.

Second, you use creative thinking techniques to develop novel solutions. Many approaches are possible here – in the following sections I outline the three I have used successfully with leadership teams.

Related worlds (easy)

A relatively easy exercise is to think outside your industry to find useful parallels. You can use related worlds to start thinking about possible options with the following steps:

1. Clearly state the problem you're trying to solve.
2. With the group, create a list of other people, industries or situations where a similar problem has been solved before.
3. Examine their solutions and identify what you can bring back to your industry and your problem.
4. Work these ideas up into one or more viable solutions.

Assumption challenge (moderate difficulty)

Break free from needless conventions and try an assumption challenge by working through the following steps:

1. Clearly state the problem you're trying to solve.
2. With the group, create a list of assumptions and conventions that apply to this problem.
3. Assumption by assumption, see what happens if you break an assumption or convention and do something different or even the opposite. Many of the options that come from this process will be dead-ends, but you'll be surprised how much innovation can come from questioning your ingrained assumptions.
4. Identify one or more viable options, flesh out the details, and state how you might test them.

Random word (advanced technique)

All new ideas come from the collision of two or more existing ideas. Therefore, taking your current situation and colliding with a wide range of other ideas can lead to novel solutions.

Try the following steps:

1. Flick through a dictionary and land your finger on a random word. Let's say you land on the word 'dinosaur'.
2. Write that word in the middle of a whiteboard.
3. Have the group shout out word associations until you have around a dozen words on the board. For example, dinosaur could have the associations old, T-rex, eggs, *Jurassic Park* and so on.
4. Then have the group work independently to solve your business problem by making connections with the words on the board. For example, continuing the dinosaur association:
   a. 'Old': Can we borrow an old idea to solve our problem? What might that be?
   b. 'T-Rex': Makes me think of being aggressive; what would a more aggressive approach to our problem look like?
   c. '*Jurassic Park*': Makes me think of movies; what if the solution was to get a new director? Or develop a content strategy?

I refer to these techniques as *deliberately thinking differently*. They benefit from some common approaches to facilitating the group, which I discuss in the following section.

FACILITATING DIVERGENCE

To encourage divergent thinking in your leadership team, first allow some solo thinking time and small group time – don't just have 'all hands' discussions. Because some people work better on their own, or in pairs, you'll get more divergent solutions if you allow these different spaces. Then bring the team back together to have a dialogue and build out the solutions.

Second, make sure the options you create are drawn up and fleshed out. I recommend putting each idea onto one page, giving it a catchy name, and fleshing out how it works. Otherwise, you end up with what I call 'braincrumbs' – crumbs of ideas which, when you revisit them a day or two later, no longer make sense.

Creative thinking like this is rare in leadership teams. The expectation of leaders is that they are serious, analytical and considered. The idea of riffing on the word 'dinosaur', for example, to solve an IT-related problem can be uncomfortable.

....

If you can create an environment where creative thinking is encouraged, you'll find it takes the leadership team to a new level. Leadership team meetings can be energising, innovative, creative. Who knew?

....

This is just a quick introduction to creative-thinking techniques. The primary route to getting more ideas from your team is to unlock their cognitive diversity. 'Deliberately thinking differently' can be considered your second strategy. For further reading, I recommend *Sticky Wisdom: How to Start a Creative Revolution at Work* by Dave Allan, Matt Kingdon, Kris Murrin and Daz Rudkin.

Compare your options side by side

As outlined earlier in this chapter, fire-fighters think up one option and play it out in their mind. If they think it will work, they go with it. If not, they then select the next option to play out. This is serial decision-making, and it's also common in business.

The alternative is to compare options simultaneously, and I've written about the benefits of having more than one option in this chapter – decisions succeed more often and can be made more quickly.

Considering your two (or more) options simultaneously, side by side, is a crucial step you'll need to take to get the benefits.

German researchers Georg Gemünden and Jürgen Hauschildt tracked the detailed records of decision-making in the leadership team of a mid-sized business, publishing their findings in the *European Journal of Operational Research*. They found 83 decisions where they could see how many alternatives were considered. Of these:

- 5 per cent had three new options on the table

- 55 per cent had two new options on the table
- 40 per cent had one new option on the table.

They were able to track the long-term outcomes across these three types. Of the 40 per cent of one-option decisions, only 6 per cent had very good outcomes. Of the 60 per cent of decisions with two or more new options, 40 per cent had very good outcomes. That's a sizeable uplift, which you will want to get your hands on.

BE CLEAR ON YOUR SELECTION PROCESS TO CONVERGE ON A SOLUTION

In most leadership teams, it's not apparent how the team should pick between options. As a team discussion unfolds, people bring in different factors to compare the options. Or they make comments in favour or against specific options. All sorts of hidden incentives, varying perspectives and different approaches are in play when it comes to making the decision. It may even feel like you are 'speaking different languages'.

Many decision-making approaches are available to guide you to decide between two or more options. And yet most leadership teams rely on a process roughly as follows:

1. Let's discuss it until we feel like making a decision.
2. We'll work out the rules as we go.
3. We can introduce new options or criteria at any moment.

Instead of this 'ad hoc' process, I recommend having some clear principles in place to help your leadership team consider the available options and then converge on a solution.

Define your success criteria

If your problem is clearly defined and you have two or more options to consider, then logic dictates you should name some dimensions to compare them on. You can do so using the ICE model. This stands for:

- *Impact:* If we take this approach and it works, what impact will it have?

- **C**onfidence: If we take this approach, what is the chance it will work?
- **E**ase: If we take this approach, how easy will it be?

The method requires you to rate each option on the three factors, and then multiply the three ratings together to obtain an expected outcome. You then pick the option with the highest expected outcome.

Make the options concrete and comparable

Whichever criteria you compare your options by, the ideas need to be presented in an easily comparable way. In practice, that means having them well fleshed out, so the details are clear and easy to judge. Depending on your organisation and the importance of the issue, that could mean anything between a one-page sketch and a full business case.

It's even possible to assign a 'red team and a blue team' to work up the two different options and make a case for them.

Consider option one thoroughly and then consider option two

Systems such as de Bono's Six Hat Thinking and venture capital firm Kleiner Perkins' Balance Sheet approach advise leadership teams to consider all the pros and cons of option one before weighing all the pros and cons of option two. (For more information on the Balance Sheet approach, see 'How we do it: Three executives reflect on strategic decision making', in *McKinsey Quarterly*.)

This process is similar to interviewing a candidate for a job. You thoroughly interview option one before interviewing option two. You're still comparing the options side by side (as outlined earlier in this chapter), but you're assessing the first option fully before moving to the second.

In *Thinking, Fast and Slow*, behavioural economist Daniel Kahneman further recommends rating each option on one criterion at a time. If using the ICE model, that would mean discussing the *impact* of option one and rating it out of ten. You would then review the *confidence* rating, before finally reviewing the *ease* rating. This approach is designed to offset the 'halo effect', where we give better ratings on all dimensions to the option we subconsciously prefer.

Surface your gut feel

In chapter 5, I drew on De Bono and Kahneman's work to suggest asking your leadership team members to state their gut feel on each option *before* discussing the pros and cons. Kahneman went further than this in his work, suggesting that you ask team members for their gut feel *after* they have rated each option. He found that when this was applied to picking candidates to be army officers, the final gut feel ratings were as accurate as computing their ratings on the criteria.

Chapter summary

Most decisions are made with just one new option on the table – that is, should we stay as we are, or make move *x*? This can be suboptimal in terms of decision effectiveness, and can also lead to slower decisions, paradoxically.

As the leader, you want to promote divergent thinking. That means unlocking your team's natural cognitive diversity, as well as using creative-thinking approaches, to generate at least two well-defined new options.

Facilitating your discussions using diamond-shaped thinking will help you balance your team's different thinking styles and come to a wise decision in good time.

Take action
Facilitate some divergent thinking with the following:

· Push for one extra alternative before you make a decision. Ella Baché CEO Pippa Hallas encourages her team to come to her with one well-defined problem, three viable

---

options, and one recommendation. She calls this the 1-3-1 approach.
- Set clear expectations in your meetings: define the problem well, spend the first half generating options and then spend the second half converging on a decision. That's diamond-shaped thinking.
- Use creative-thinking techniques to unlock a new level of productivity and enjoyment in your leadership team, as well as develop more innovative ideas and solutions.

Next

You've developed some powerful options. In the next chapter, we explore how to think further ahead – how might your ideas and decisions play out?

8

Further.
Thinking further ahead to make wise decisions.

A TITANIC DECISION

I'm standing on the prow of the Manly Ferry on my way to work. We're gliding between the Sydney Opera House on one side and the Harbour Bridge on the other, when it hit me.

'Why don't I leave my job in advertising and start a business helping people make better decisions?'

I studied psychology and decision-making at university – I'd even written a paper on it (published in the *Journal of Thinking and Reasoning* in 1997, called 'Probability and choice in the selection task').

Back to my life in Sydney, and I was doing more reading than writing – and I'd just read a book describing Google's history. They'd made a fortune helping people find information. But that didn't mean people found it easy to *use* the information to make difficult decisions. Wouldn't it help the world if people could make better decisions? And wouldn't companies pay for that too?

That was a Friday morning in February 2013. I felt a rush of energy and confidence. 'This is a great idea! I'll resign as soon as I get into work.'

Seconds later: 'No, let's not rush. If I'm going to help others make good decisions, I need to use my decision-making tips on myself.'

First, I created three criteria to choose the right next path. I wanted something that would suit my values, use my strengths and pay the mortgage.

Second, I made sure I had three options – not just 'stay' or 'go'. So I wrote down, 'fix the current job; get a new job; start a decision-making advisory'. And then I evaluated each option on the three criteria.

Sensible stuff so far.

The third step was not so obvious. I needed to burst my bubble of confidence and see what happened. I needed an external perspective.

On the following Saturday night, I asked three people for dinner – three people whose opinions I valued and who had some relevant expertise. I shared my business plan with them using a few slides presented on my TV over cheese and wine. And then I asked them this question: 'Imagine we've fast-forwarded to 12 months in the future and my business has failed. Looking back from then, why did it fail?'

This approach is called a *premortem*, popularised by Gary Klein in his *Harvard Business Review* article 'Performing a project premortem'. It's a form of prospective hindsight that, as researchers highlighted in 'Back to the future: Temporal perspective in the explanation of events', has been shown to improve people's ability to find reasons for future outcomes by 30 per cent.

My dinner companions took to the task with relish.

'You fell ill and had no sick pay.'

'You couldn't get access to key decision-makers.'

'You weren't able to work at home and got distracted all the time.'

I captured all of their ideas, a number of which I hadn't thought of myself.

The next day I adjusted my business plan accordingly, feeling a more realistic sense of confidence. I added a 12-month timeline to prove it could work. I wrote down a plan B, C and D.

Two days later, on a Tuesday morning eight years ago, I walked into the CEO's office and resigned.

Put the Kool-Aid on ice

Did the decision get a good outcome? Yes: my role now fits my values, and it uses my strengths, and it has paid the mortgage for the last eight years.

Was the decision process effective? Well, this is a different question – a poorly made decision can get a good outcome, and a well-made decision can have a bad outcome. I believe the creation of criteria, generation of multiple options and premortem did make for an effective decision-making process.

The critical steps I've just outlined are also vital for leadership teams before they press 'go' on a project.

Let's say you've thought deeply on a problem (as advised in chapter 6), and you've developed a range of options and aligned on one preferred way forward (chapter 7).

Something strange can happen to your leadership team at this point. You get the Kool-Aid out, and pass it round. Everyone takes a sip and feels more and more confident about the plan. It's intoxicating.

This overconfidence can be amplified by groups. Your group may get *more* overconfident than I was that Friday morning on the ferry, about to resign half an hour after coming up with a business idea.

Like me, you need to hit pause and say, 'No, let's not rush.' Put the Kool-Aid on ice while you take a breath and make sure you have thought about how your plan could play out and what might go wrong.

Groups can amplify biases

The reason to take a pause is because of three cognitive biases that can lead groups to become overconfident in their decisions and plans.

Cognitive biases are ways of thinking that help us make quick decisions – but also lead to predictable errors in certain situations.

An example is the confirmation bias. You have an idea and then look selectively for evidence that supports it, ignoring counter-evidence. Then you use the selective evidence you've gathered to support your belief.

Scientists have studied many cognitive biases and how they affect business decisions. In 'The case for behavioural strategy', professor Dan Lovallo and McKinsey director Oliver Sibony categorised the biases most relevant to business leaders into four groups.

The first group is 'action-oriented biases', which can be summarised as follows:

- *Excessive optimism:* Individuals overestimate the upside of their plan and underestimate the downside risks.
- *Overconfidence:* Individuals overestimate their own, and their organisation's, skill levels relative to others – leading to overconfidence that they can affect future outcomes.
- *Competitor neglect:* Individuals make plans without factoring in how competitors may act or react.

These action-oriented biases are the ones your leadership team needs to address in the moment between deciding and acting.

Each of them is a problem for an individual leader. But worse is to come. In *Wiser: Getting Beyond Groupthink to Make Groups Smarter,* Cass Sunstein and Reid Hastie highlight how groups can *amplify* each of these biases.

One form of excessive optimism is known as the *planning fallacy:* when planning a project, we tend to overestimate its impact and underestimate the time it will take, and the budget needed. One example is the Sydney Opera House – which I was ferrying past earlier in the chapter. The Opera House went fourteen times over its original budget and took ten years longer than planned to build.

The planning fallacy is commonly amplified by group discussion, as outlined by Roger Buehler, Deanna Messervey and Dale Wesley Griffin in 'Collaborative planning and prediction'. This can be from an infectious optimism and the tendency to focus on 'planning for success'.

Groups can also amplify overconfidence, as argued by Janet Sniezek and Rebecca Henry in 'Accuracy and confidence in group judgment'. If you ask the individuals for their confidence in an outcome and then ask them to discuss and agree on a *group* confidence level, the group's confidence is often higher than the individuals' average. The group discussion creates more overconfidence.

The proof that these optimism and confidence levels are excessive comes from tracking the success rate of large projects and transformation initiatives. According to McKinsey's 2015 survey 'How to beat the transformation odds':

> Today, just 26 per cent of respondents say the transformations they're most familiar with have been very or completely successful at both improving performance and equipping the organisation to sustain improvements over time.

To avoid this level of failure and disappointment, you can take a breath between decision and action. You can pause to think about how the project might play out, what might go wrong, and adjust the plan accordingly.

Put your plan back on ICE

In chapter 7, I outline how to assess the probable outcome of two options by considering their impact, confidence and ease (ICE). As shown in table 8.1, these three criteria can also serve as a useful guide as you move from decision to action.

In the remainder of this chapter, I provide more information on the techniques mentioned in table 8.1, including running a premortem and using experimentation. I also introduce my change checklist cards, and run through how to use them. These techniques are all guides to help your team think further ahead. Doing so will help you harness the power of perspective – and a healthy dose of pessimism.

Table 8.1: Using Impact, Confidence and Ease (ICE) to recognise and reduce overconfidence bias

	Bias	What we want	How we get it
Impact	Teams are excessively optimistic of the impact of their plans	A more accurate estimate of the impact	Consider a premortem: how might our plan fail?
Confidence	Teams are overconfident in their ability to deliver the required actions	Learn by experimenting, get to plan B	Run a test-and-learn experiment before going all-in
Ease	Teams underestimate the time, money and effort required to deliver a project	Commit to a more robust plan of action	Use the change checklist cards

....

Remember – the better you work together as a team, the more risk you create for groupthink and amplifying the group's biases. The solution is to disrupt your thinking.

....

The tools and techniques outlined in this chapter provide ways to identify and disrupt cognitive biases.

PROSPECTIVE HINDSIGHT: THE PREMORTEM

Ryan leads a professional services firm called LCA Consultancy. Ryan was about to 'offshore' all his administration work to a company in the Philippines. At this moment, between decision and action, he was seated with six other leaders from other businesses at a workshop. The group was asked to use the premortem technique described at the start of this chapter on a live business decision. Here's what they did:

1. Ryan described the plan for a few minutes to the other leaders.

2. He asked the critical question: 'Imagine it's 12 months' time and we're back here, and I'm telling you it was a disaster. Can you tell me why it failed?'
3. For five minutes, each person wrote a long list of potential reasons onto their notepad – in silence.
4. Ryan asked each person for their single top reason.
5. Then he collated all the other answers and grouped them.
6. Finally, he highlighted the reasons he wanted to address with a revised plan.

The whole exercise took 15 minutes. In my workshops, senior leaders often highlight this technique as providing significant value in minimal time. They also appeared to enjoy the mental challenge of filling in the gaps in Ryan's story.

The psychology of premortems

Let's repeat the potential benefits: a 30 per cent greater ability to generate reasons for failure, compared to a standard approach of 'let's look at your plan and assess its risks'.

Why does the premortem work so well?

Filling in the gaps in the story

Humans are excellent at creating stories from simple facts. If I say, 'The dog ran into the road,' you can, without much effort at all, turn the words into a story in your head, visualising why it happened, what happened next and how people felt. You can even see the road and the dog in your mind – all from six words. In fact, it's hard *not* to visualise the scene and play out the story in your mind's eye.

(As an aside, a famous example of this is the six-word story sometimes attributed to Ernest Hemingway: 'For sale: baby shoes, never worn'.)

Suppose you simply ask people to do a risk assessment of your plan. In that case, people use their critical thinking skills to identify commonly known business risks such as cashflow, internal buy-in and product development timelines.

Instead, if you use a premortem to leverage their story-building skills and their imagination, their answers tend to be much more practical and people-oriented.

> **Working backwards from the moment of failure is more powerful than thinking about the plan as it is today and thinking forward.**

Promoting dissent and divergence

In the Ryan example, you'll notice that he asked the six leaders to think on their own first. This generates far more divergent views. After 5 minutes, a pool of up to 50 potential reasons was ready to be discussed (although many likely overlapped). If this were run as a group discussion, you'd still be discussing the first, probably obvious, reason after five minutes.

You can also see that each person was asked to give their top reason first. The rationale for this is if person A gives all of theirs, then person B gives all of theirs, and so on, by the time you get to person E, most of theirs have already been said, so they feel they contributed less.

Lastly, you can also choose to dial up creative thinking with this technique. For example, in one premortem a participant said, 'The launch in Melbourne may fail because a massive meteorite blows up the whole city'. On its own, that is not helpful. But it caused another team member to say, 'That makes me think – have we factored in all the insurance costs of launching?'

This is a useful example of why allowing divergent thinking has value, and also of the following principle: It's not true that 'no idea is a bad idea'.

> **We all have bad ideas every day. It's just we need an environment in which people feel safe to share their bad ideas. Bad ideas can be the stepping stones to good ideas.**

This divergence and dissent – the ability to be negative about a plan – has two surprising outcomes:

- First, teams seem to enjoy it. Time and again, I've seen that loosening them from the shackles of being polite, professional and constructive – even for 15 minutes – turns out to be fun.
- Second, 90 per cent of the time it leads to the plan owner feeling more confident about their plan. 'If that's the worst that can happen, then I have a few tweaks I can make, and I feel more realistically confident it will work.'

The premortem is a great way to unlock the collective intelligence of your leadership team.

The pre-parade

If you're running a premortem, you have an extra option: to run a pre-parade. This is similar to a premortem, but you ask your team to imagine the plan is a wild success, and to tell the story, from 12 months' time, of *why it was a success*.

If you have a large leadership team, you can divide this process between two groups. Have one group run the premortem and the other group run the pre-parade.

The pre-parade has some important outcomes. It can help you work out which aspects of your plan are most important, or even overlooked.

If the team comes up with the idea that 'The Melbourne launch was a wild success because two competitors also opened up at the same time and grew the whole category with their advertising spend,' it may reveal an overlooked part of your plan: the opportunity to grow the category or to collaborate with competitors.

Be emotionally intelligent with your premortems

Premortems are a proven way to help a team think about the future more accurately. And they can be a great energiser for the team.

However, you do need to watch out for one aspect. If the team has signs of conflict, or if the idea in question has one owner, then you may want to introduce the premortem carefully. Cassie doesn't want to feel her pet project is being attacked on all sides.

If you have set up an emotionally intelligent leadership team and generated ideas that everyone owns, you won't find this problem. You'll find the premortem becomes a regular part of your team meetings and, in fact, a positive contributor to the team's emotional intelligence.

EXPERIMENTING TO COUNTERACT OVERCONFIDENCE

What's happening when a leadership team falls prey to overconfidence? Let's revisit the definition.

Teams overestimate their own, and their organisation's, skill levels relative to others – leading to overconfidence that they can affect future outcomes.

The last three words are worth noting. Overconfidence often leads to you and your teaming thinking they can 'affect future outcomes.'

This type of overconfidence leads teams to dive headfirst into a project because they believe in their abilities. They think if something doesn't go quite right, they can change course. No need to dip a toe in the water, they'll learn as they go and adjust plans as necessary. 'Let's just dive in'.

....
In the moments between decision and action, I encourage you to pause on the edge of the pool before you dive in.
....

As a team, you should ask:

- 'Can we put a toe in the water first?'
- 'How about we drop a stone in and see how deep it is?'
- 'How about one of us jumps in before everybody else follows?'

This can feel like an anticlimax, because you just made a decision – you can see the promised land. The future outcomes are fully visible in your mind's eye. And you know what you need to do. 'Let's just dive in'.

And sometimes you do need to dive in and make it work. But, more often than not, you can put a toe in first to check the temperature. This will allow you to calibrate your confidence and learn what really works.

Remember – according to the McKinsey survey 'How to beat the transformation odds', only 26 per cent of transformation efforts work.

And in *Getting to Plan B*, John Mullins and Randy Komisar report their findings from an informal survey of entrepreneurs. When asked if their original business plan had worked, two-thirds said 'no'. In fact, they said, they had re-started their companies, nearly three times each.

Faced with these odds, responsible leadership teams need to consider whether they can run experiments, do test-and-learns, build prototypes or develop minimal viable products.

Suppose you can develop an experiment that allows you to test the key hypotheses behind your plan. In doing so, you will develop a much more realistic sense of confidence in your organisation's ability to deliver the results that your plan promises.

As an example, your leadership team could test two hypotheses:

1. *The value hypothesis:* Does your proposed new product deliver value that customers love?
2. *The growth hypothesis:* Does your proposed new approach to growing the customer base work?

If you are in a large corporate, however, your leadership team's plans may be quite different from this. So when can you run an experiment before diving in to implementation with your team?

When to experiment

Scott Cook, CEO of Intuit, is a proponent of bringing experimentation into large corporates as a core competency of leadership. As Cook emphasises about experimentation (in 'Scott Cook's recipe for lean experiments' on nextbigwhat.com):

> The biggest impact is on decision making. It's a huge cultural shift for the leaders to let go of decision making. Indeed, most have grown up on the 'fact' that leadership is primarily about being decisive!

The classic scenarios to run experiments and tests in include:

- *Product:* Testing new products and services. Can you prototype it and test it with real consumers rather than focus groups and market research?
- *Marketing:* A/B testing of two variations on a webpage. Continual testing to optimise conversions.
- *People initiatives:* Testing new recruitment, training or retention initiatives. Do they have an impact; are they scalable?
- *Systems:* Testing new systems before full roll-out. Will the impact be as high, and the costs come in as forecast?

For these projects and plans – and many more – it's possible to develop a test that contributes valuable data and helps you refine the plan to be more realistic.

How to run an experiment

In this section, I provide a brief overview of running experiments. This can be supplemented by many excellent books on experimentation, including *The Lean Startup* by Eric Ries and *Getting to Plan B* by John Mullins and Randy Komisar.

Here are the steps in running an experiment:

1. Make experimentation a positive behavioural norm in your culture.
2. Be clear on the strategy and the problem you're trying to solve; what are your goals?
3. Develop a plan (plan A) you believe can solve your problem.
4. Identify the key hypotheses you need to test to see if plan A will solve the problem – for example, the value hypothesis and growth hypothesis (refer to earlier in this chapter).
5. Identify the amount of data you need to capture to make this a robust test.
6. Build a test or minimal viable product at the lowest possible budget.
7. Test the plan in realistic circumstances (ideally with real customers, not market research groups).
8. Use a dashboard to track the results (see chapter 10 for more on this).

9. Once you have enough results, assess plan A against the hypotheses, and either scale up plan A or use what you've learnt to develop a plan B that is more likely to hit your original strategic goals.

Does this approach to experimentation feel weak or brave to you?

When your team is ready to dive into the pool, suddenly asking them to follow a nine-step process such as this will deflate them. It will feel weak.

If, however, you and your team have set the expectation that you will run experiments, it's not only brave but also smart.

This process allows you to tackle the group's overconfidence, and create the conditions for them to learn more quickly than their competitors.

....

If you can learn more quickly than your competitors, it doesn't matter where you are today: you'll win in the long run.

....

Putting a toe in the water is a brave move

To illustrate this approach, a multinational media organisation called MJT wanted to allow its customers to buy ads themselves without going through a salesperson. For several years, they'd asked their large CRM provider to build the required systems. Their quote to do so had come in as many millions of dollars. Based on the budget, MJT had never committed to the innovation. They'd stood on the edge of the pool watching other people swim happily – and not dived in.

Then, a prototyping company approached them and said, 'We can build you a prototype in 30 days: a working model where your customers can buy one product, one type of ad, in one geographic market. But it will be fully functional.'

In other words, they were offering a 'test-and-learn' option. MJT rolled the dice and ran the experiment. It worked. From there, they built out the whole e-commerce self-service platform.

This example shows us that experiments can encourage appropriate levels of bravery (often lacking in larger corporates, due to incentives implicitly favouring safety over risk – even when 'courage' is written into the corporate values) and much faster speeds of innovation.

Even if MJT had stumped up the budget to pay the large CRM provider to roll out an entire system at once, it would likely have been slower and less successful.

COMMIT TO A ROBUST PLAN USING A CHANGE CHECKLIST

In *Thinking, Fast and Slow*, Daniel Kahneman, Nobel-prize winning expert on cognitive biases, relates the following story.

He was collaborating with several other experts to write a textbook about judgement and decision-making. A year into the process, they had finalised the book's outline and written the first two chapters. Meeting to plan the next steps, Kahneman asked the group to estimate how long it would take to complete the book. They all wrote down their estimates in private (to reduce groupthink). Their estimates ranged from one and a half to two and a half years.

One of the team happened to have seen other groups write text-books, so Kahneman asked him, 'How long did those teams take?' The answer: 40 per cent never finished; and all of the others took between seven and ten years.

This group – of judgement and decision-making experts – chose to fall straight into what's known as the planning fallacy and ignored the expert's external estimates. They carried on as if two years was about right.

They finished the book eight years later.

Projects are rarely as easy as they look

Underneath the planning fallacy is a *narrowness of perspective*.

Imagine you are planning a significant, transformative initiative. You could fail to appreciate how the required transformation looks to the people in the organisation. Transformations are mainly about people. If they don't have the skills, motivation and resources, you'll run into trouble

You might fail to recognise the project's complexity or its unin-tended consequences (its deep links to other parts of the system). These can introduce significant cost and delays into a project.

You may fail to consider the range of external factors that could affect the project. On their own, each may be unlikely (for example, weather events, economic crises, change of ownership or new government regulations). But, put together, chance will suggest at least one of them *will* happen. In other words, projects rely on luck – to some extent – and all the cards are unlikely to fall your way.

Playing the change cards to make your plan more robust

In the moment between decision and action, it can help the leadership team to see a checklist – one that prompts more robust thinking. This thinking could consider, for example, what will it take to make this project a success? How confident can we be?

To help provide this checklist, I developed the 24 Change Checklist Cards shown in figure 8.1. Your leadership team can lay out the checklist cards and pick out the ones you believe are most critical to make your plans work. This leads to productive discussion among the team: how much effort will be required to support this change?

The cards were first drawn from several excellent sources about change management, including *Switch*, by Dan and Chip Heath; *Influencer* by Joseph Grenny, Kerry Patterson, David Maxfield, Ron McMillan and Al Switzler; *The Heart of Change* by John Kotter; and McKinsey's 'How to beat the transformation odds' survey. I then refined the cards through use with numerous leadership teams in different industries. The 24 cards fall into three categories: rational plays, emotional plays, and make-it-easier plays. These categories correspond to Jonathan Haidt's 'elephant and rider' psychological theory of change, which he outlines in *The Happiness Hypothesis*.

In this theory, you imagine asking your team to make a change or commit to a plan. Their emotional reactions to your request are processed by a large part of their brain, the emotional brain. It is more ancient and more concerned with fight or flight reactions. Although mainly subconscious, reactions from this part of the brain drive a lot of our feelings about change.

A smaller portion of your brain processes your rational response to the request. This is the more recently evolved part of the human brain, which consciously processes our thoughts. It asks, 'What do

I need to do? Why is this important? How does it fit with everything else you're asking me to do already?'

The emotional brain is the elephant, because it is much larger. The rational brain is the rider, the one who directs the elephant – but only if the elephant wants to move in the same direction.

This means your first strategy before committing to a plan is to play some of the cards that motivate the elephant, the emotional brain. Your second strategy is to play some of the cards that direct the rider, telling the rational brain precisely what's expected.

There's a third strategy: you also need to make change as easy as possible. Ideally, using the new behaviour should be immediately easier than using the old behaviour. This is hard to achieve – adopting a new behaviour almost always involves at least a small hurdle. Nonetheless, the leadership team and project owners need to make the transition as easy as possible. This means playing cards that 'clear the elephant's path'.

One sales leadership team used the cards to make a robust plan. They needed to transform their sales team from an inbound order-taking focus to an outbound customer-finding focus. The team laid out the cards on the board room table. Each team member picked two or three cards they thought were important to discuss. Significant issues were raised: were all members of the executive leadership team 100 per cent on board with the plan? Who might resist the change? How could they motivate people with the urgency of the change? The change checklist cards allow a leadership team to stress test a plan before diving into the pool.

Creating the exact blow-by-blow plan before committing to an idea is unnecessary – and can even be counterproductive according to Eric Ries in *The Lean Startup*. However, running through this change checklist can provide a realistic sense of how difficult or easy the plan might be. And the cards can be used again when it's time to make the full project plan.

In part IV of this book, I extend this future thinking into practical action, addressing how to make plans, track progress and learn from our actions.

Figure 8.1: The 24 Change Checklist Cards

1. Visible exec alignment: Get the executive team in true alignment on the need for change, and role-model behaviour change	2. Decision rights: Be clear on who owns which decision	3. Harness influencers: Get key influencers' buy-in first; don't try to get everyone on board
4. Feel the change: Create emotional appeal by dramatising the consequences of changing (or not)	5. Let them be heard: Allow staff to provide feedback and input to change strategy and plans	6. Tangible vision: Ensure staff are able to see themselves in the future version of the company
7. Urgency: Be clear on the urgency for change & the consequences of not changing	8. Specific destination: Create a very specific endpoint that feels achievable; e.g. +20% profit by Dec 31	9. Critical behaviours: Focus on the behaviours critical to achieve change
10. Show me my KPIs: What does the change mean for me, and what are my new KPIs?	11. Celebrate small wins: Deliberately create and celebrate small successes; ensure people get feedback on progress	12. Remove obstacles: Be seen to empower staff by removing obstacles to change – people, systems, structures
13. Skills development: Provide training & coaching to support changing behaviours	14. Real change today: Chunk the change down and apply changes to real work as soon as possible, don't keep it abstract	15. Bright spots: Examine where change has gone right before, and replicate the reasons
16. Social pressure: Apply peer pressure and competition by showcasing successes from other departments	17. Social ability: Encourage peers to help each other learn and apply new behaviours	18. Punishment: If necessary, call out examples of disruptive or divisive behaviour
19. Call on purpose: Relate the changes to your company's purpose, mission or vision	20. Eliminate vested interests: Identify and eliminate the reasons not to change	21. Economic benefit: Spell out the economic benefits of change in a compelling rational argument
22. Project management: Have a concrete step-by-step plan for the change, and frequent check-ins	23. The scorecard: Be seen to measure change and regularly report back on progress	24. Test and learn: Forget the big strategy, try some new approaches on a smaller scale; measure their success

Chapter summary

When your team decides on an idea, they are likely to be overconfident and excessively optimistic about their plans.

Recognise that, in the moments between decision and action – similar to the three days between coming up with my business idea and resigning from my job – you and your leadership team should *put the Kool-Aid on ice*.

Question the *impact*: will the project have as much impact as you think?

Question your *confidence*: will your skills be able to deliver the impact?

Question the *ease* of the project: what haven't you and your team thought about that the project will need?

A healthy dose of realism – even pessimism – can go a long way before you dive into a project.

Take action

Use the three methods from this chapter to be more *realistically confident* in your plans:

- Plan to fail using a premortem, similar to what Ryan did, and what I ran through during the dinner party at my house.
- Put a toe in the water instead of diving in. Design an experiment using the nine-step process outlined in the section 'How to run an experiment'.
- Run a checklist to make sure your plan is robust, using my Change Checklist Cards to discuss elements of successful change projects. (For a set of the cards, go to robpyne. online/unlock.)

Next

You've thought about impact, confidence and ease and made a decision. Now you can turn to the third type of intelligence. That's the team's practical intelligence – how to turn your ideas and decisions into real-world impact.

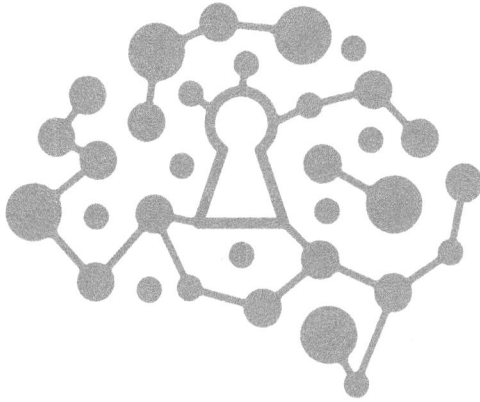

PART IV

UNLOCKING THE TEAM'S
PRACTICAL INTELLIGENCE

I used to have a colleague named Jamie. He was highly intelligent, and was well-liked and inspiring to his team. But he was always late for everything, and he never seemed able to sort his life out. His job was always out-of-control busy, details slipped through the cracks, projects were started but never finished.

For a time, I was puzzled: how can someone so intelligent not work out how to run projects and deliver to deadlines?

One day, I realised that intellectual intelligence is entirely unrelated to common sense – which I now call practical intelligence.

In my work with leadership teams, I have noticed the same disconnect. When a group of intelligent and successful individuals come together, there is not only no guarantee they will be collectively able to solve problems, but also no telling how successful they will be at delivering on their plans. The answers to the following are unclear:

- Will they turn their ideas into robust plans?
- Will they be able to motivate others to take action?
- Will they be accountable for delivering their key initiatives and projects?
- Will their leadership team meetings make any practical impact?

Think about the leadership teams of two competing organisations – say, Uber and Lyft. Winning in a competitive market is arguably much more about execution than it is to do with a ground-breaking business idea. Copying each other's ideas is easier than winning through execution.

My research has identified three aspects of practical intelligence on which leadership teams can focus.

In chapter 9, I explore the discipline of planning and how to turn your ideas into a roadmap.

In chapter 10, I outline useful techniques to track your progress.

And in chapter 11, I uncover the reasons your leadership team should practice reflecting and refuelling, using a 'pit stop' strategy.

As founder and CEO of Dell Technologies, Michael Dell, says:

> Ideas are a commodity. Execution of them is not.

9

Plans.
Making your goals stick.

TWO OCTOPUSES

Imagine two octopuses are competing for control of an attractive patch of rock shelf.

Octopus A wants the rock shelf. After all, it's got some great feeding opportunities and good defences. But he hasn't worked out how to win it, or a plan for what he needs to do. So, he just keeps shouting at everyone how much he wants it. 'It's mine.' Occasionally he lurches at the other octopus. But his brain hasn't communicated his intent to his legs. So his legs get confused and don't manage to mount a proper attack.

Octopus B recognises that each of an octopus's legs has its own brain (true story) and can act independently of the head. So, he works out he needs to send clear instructions on how to attack, and what precisely to do. He also knows that octopus legs have short memories and need a regular reminder of the goals.

Which octopus does your organisation resemble?

Leadership teams face a few hurdles in my experience regarding the seemingly straightforward task of goal-setting:

- They first need to navigate the difference between 'being', 'doing' and 'arriving' goals.
- Then they need to translate goals into projects and actions, spaced over time.
- These projects need to be realistically prioritised against the available resources.
- And, finally, goals need to be connected to the organisation's day-to-day behaviours.

All four elements are necessary for your team to develop 'sticky goals': goals that are widely understood and consistently actioned. Goals that actually make an impact – which is the goal of having goals, right?

SETTING THE RIGHT GOALS

If you develop a strategy or agree on a plan, someone in your leadership team will quickly agitate for you to create specific, detailed goals. They might say you need SMART goals (specific, measurable, achievable, realistic, time-bound). Or they might want to draw up OKRs, as popularised by Google (objectives and key results). Or perhaps OGSMs (objectives, goals, strategies and measures).

When it comes to working with leadership teams, you need to go beyond these acronyms for a slightly ironic reason: they are all merely descriptive. They're focused on how to write a goal, and on the contents or elements of the goal. They don't focus on the outcome you want from your goals – that they make an impact.

I've seen many times that unless you pay close attention to your goals, you are significantly reducing the chance of delivering your strategy.

Leadership teams are often confounded by two hurdles in particular. But they needn't be hard work – as I show in the following sections.

The first hurdle: what matters?

To start building better goals, the first hurdle leadership teams face is selecting the right parts of the business to measure.

A CEO told me, 'We grew 60 per cent last year, but we don't know exactly what we did that drove that growth. We have ideas, but no certainty.' This CEO was struggling with the organisation's forward strategy – to get 60 per cent growth again – because his team hadn't measured key parts of the business and learnt how they affected financial outcomes.

The story illustrates two key ideas about goal setting. First, you need to clearly understand your own business model, and pick the critical parts to measure. Second, you need to develop an understanding of how these elements work together to drive the ultimate outcome, such as profit.

Think of this as being like the engine of your aeroplane. You need to know which are the critical parts, how they affect overall perfor- mance and how to measure their output. Do you have enough fuel? What temperature is the engine running at? Is there enough oil pressure?

When it comes to your business, I recommend building your goals by looking at your overall business model laid out on paper, perhaps by using the Business Model Canvas I discuss in chapter 6. The Business Model Canvas suggests you can break a business model into nine elements, from distribution channels to value proposi- tions. You can then measure these elements, and know how they work together – and can be tweaked – to drive different outcomes.

Organisations create, deliver and extract value

The nine elements group into three parts of your business 'engine': how you *create* value for a customer; how you *deliver* that value; and how you *extract* some of that value for yourself as profit. (This analysis of business models having three parts is informed by *The Personal MBA: Master the Art of Business*, by Josh Kaufman.)

The value creation elements are:

· Value proposition
· Customer definition
· Acquisition
· Distribution (channels)

Value delivery is based on:

- Activities
- Resources
- Partnerships

And value extraction includes:

- Revenue
- Costs

To create your set of goals, you can identify which of these areas you need to monitor most closely in order to keep your business improving. And you'll want to identify which areas are most critical to reshaping your organisation in line with your strategy.

Often you would focus on between four and six areas that you have determined are the most important to grow the business and deliver the strategy, although you could measure all nine parts of the business model. These picks are sometimes called your *key result areas* or KRAs. Aligning the leadership team on these KRAs can be hugely beneficial.

One leadership team I worked with had previously created five goals for their organisation: skilled people, a stronger culture, innovative products, consistent service delivery and delivery of a revenue target.

When we went through these goals in more detail, I pushed them to go back to basics and identify the key results areas – the things they needed to look at to see how well their business was running and whether they were delivering the strategy. They realised that their five draft goals included two people-related areas, and no customer areas. We were quickly able to align on a solution: put people and culture into one combined KRA, add a process goal, and add a customer goal.

Visually arranging the key result areas as a system

Once you have outlined your goals, focusing on between four and six key result areas, you can write these goals on your plan using a logical visual arrangement. The arrangement, shown in figure 9.1, is a bit like a funnel. At the top of the funnel, people deliver

Figure 9.1: An example of a set of six key results areas

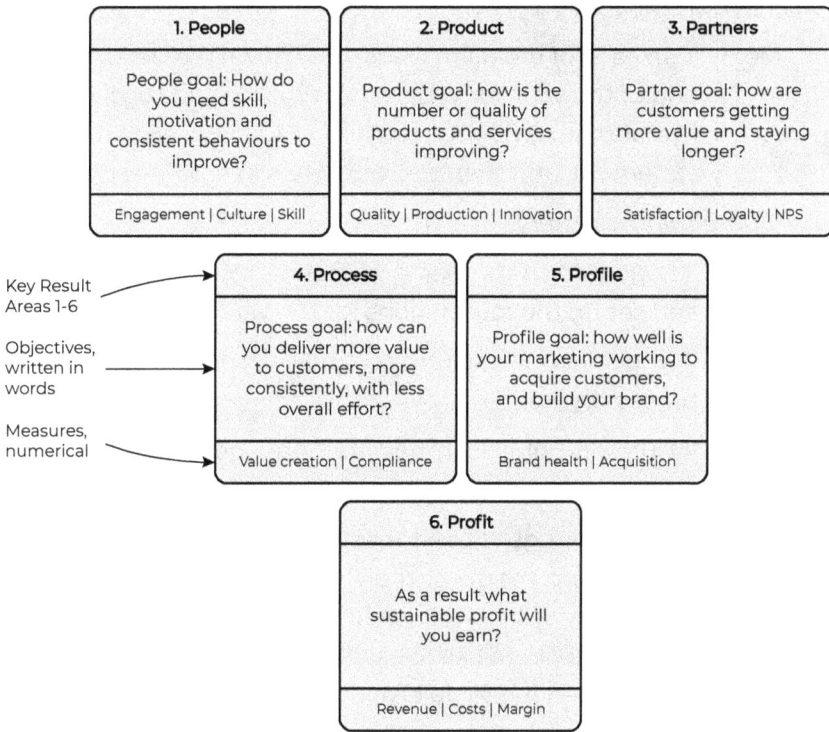

1. People	2. Product	3. Partners
People goal: How do you need skill, motivation and consistent behaviours to improve?	Product goal: how is the number or quality of products and services improving?	Partner goal: how are customers getting more value and staying longer?
Engagement | Culture | Skill	Quality | Production | Innovation	Satisfaction | Loyalty | NPS

Key Result Areas 1-6

Objectives, written in words

Measures, numerical

4. Process	5. Profile
Process goal: how can you deliver more value to customers, more consistently, with less overall effort?	Profile goal: how well is your marketing working to acquire customers, and build your brand?
Value creation | Compliance	Brand health | Acquisition

6. Profit
As a result what sustainable profit will you earn?
Revenue | Costs | Margin

products to partners. In the middle row, processes connect people to products, and profile connects products to partners. If you get all these areas working, then profit should flow out the bottom of the funnel.

Seeing this visually, as a system, makes it easier to remember (as does the alliteration within it). In my experience, this arrangement is also more motivating, because it's easier to understand how your job, and that of the leadership team, fits in to the bigger picture.

Establishing a set of key result areas is the first step. But exactly what are the goals you measure under each area?

The second hurdle: which measures?

Leadership teams often struggle with writing goals to sit under the key result areas. In particular, it's easy to confuse a goal about what you're going to *do*, with a goal of what *impact* you need to have.

To illustrate, here's the outline of a discussion I facilitated with a chief people officer and his team.

Me: 'Can each of the team leads write down the goals, for the end of the year, for your team. What would success look like, and how will you measure it? Can you write it with a statement, and then two or three metrics?'

(Some minutes later.)

Eliza: 'My goal for next year is to define my team's purpose and set up the foundations for the year after.'

Andy: 'My goal is to launch the new performance review process by April.'

Deb: 'At the end of December, staff engagement will be up from 67 per cent to 72 per cent.'

I invite you to ask your gut how it reacts to each of those. If you're like me, none of them seems entirely satisfactory. They leave me wanting more clarity. If I were in their team, I would feel disconnected from these goals. I'd like to ask, 'Why?' Or, 'How?' Or, 'When by? What do you need me to do exactly?'

....

Goals have to ladder up and down.

....

At the top of the ladder should be an arriving goal. This outlines where you are trying to get to, by when, and how you will know when you get there. Deb's goal is an arriving goal. Note that it is passive; it describes a moment in time. It does not detail the journey. As a result, it can be challenging for humans to connect to and be motivated by.

Below this should be a doing goal. Andy's goal is a doing goal. You can watch out for these with goals that start with the verb 'launch' or other similar 'doing words'. Doing goals are fine, as long as they are partnered with an arriving goal. The reason? Because without an arriving goal, the metric of the doing goal is simply, 'Did you do it?' And that means it's disconnected from driving results. You goal could be to launch a new type of sneakers. You achieve this, but only sell a hundred pairs. You still hit the going goal: "to launch."

Doing goals have benefits. They are easier for people to visualise and chunk down into specific actions. They can be easier to communicate and motivate people. However, doing goals are often actually *projects* and can be taken off the list of goals.

Finally, at the bottom of the ladder, you may need a being goal, like Eliza's. Being goals describe the foundations you want to build, how you want to be – before you start doing the work and arriving at outcomes.

Being goals can also be motivating. Ideally, they are paired with a doing goal and an arriving goal – for example, we will set our foundations by being W, and then we'll do projects X and Y to arrive at Z.

You can see how these goals ladder up in the simple diagram shown in figure 9.2.

Imagine you worked at NASA in the year 1960. This arrangement of a being goal, then a doing goal, and then an arriving goal has an attractive logic that is memorable and motivating for teams.

In my experience, teams often don't feel this way when their leaders pronounce goals that focus only on arriving, such as the following:

- 'We're going to be number 1.'
- 'We're going to win awards.'
- 'We're going to double in revenue by two years' time.'

Figure 9.2: Being, doing and arriving goals

Landing
on
the moon
before the Russians — *Arriving goals*

Building a rocket — *Doing goals*

Assembling a team of experts — *Being goals*

The team struggle with 'how are we going to do that?' and 'what do I need to do?'

So, underneath your key result areas, you can add one achieving goal (these are vital) supported by a doing goal and perhaps a being goal (you don't always need to specify all three levels).

For example, under the people area, you could end up with this:

People

Our goal is to improve the capability of our people, and the positive impact of our culture:

- Capability: Complete a learning needs analysis by March and show a 10 per cent improvement on the top three skills we need across the organisation by December, as measured by performance review data.
- Culture: Develop and launch our new values by June, and measure their impact on staff engagement, which we want to improve from 67 per cent to 72 per cent by December's engagement survey.

CONNECTING GOALS TO THE INDIVIDUAL

Perhaps you and your leadership team are happy with your goal-setting system. Maybe you're good at cascading goals down to your team. Potentially you have a personal review process where KPIs are set.

In which case, you are in an absolute minority. Kaplan and Norton's paper 'The Strategy-Focused Organization', included an alarming statistic.

....

A mere 7 per cent of employees today fully understand their company's business strategies and what's expected of them in order to help achieve company goals.

....

So, when the leadership team discusses goals, you need to focus on making sure the goals turn into action, by constructing motivating, sticky goals – and then communicating them clearly and consistently.

And then you'll need to have your middle managers work with their teams to show how frontline employee behaviours and priorities need to change to deliver on these goals. An effective way to bring priorities to life is to map out all the activities needed to hit your doing and achieving goals.

Turn your goals into a visible project roadmap

Over the last 20 years, business has become more visual.

Think back to the template for a business plan from the 1990s. You probably think of a long document with multiple chapters for everything from key personnel, marketing budgets and financial metrics.

Fast-forward to the 2010s and organisations were summarising their business model on the one-page Business Model Canvas (discussed in chapter 6), showing the relationships between the nine elements of a business including key activities, cost structures and ideal customers.

And the visualisation of key ideas has continued:

- Work-in-progress (WIP) documents have turned into Kanban boards.
- Data overload has spawned data visualisation skills.
- Project plans have turned into swim lane diagrams.

And, in my case, when I develop a strategy with leadership teams, the end product is usually a one-page strategy house (see chapter 13), accompanied by a supporting narrative.

Is this a fad? Or is there a reason for it?

One possibility centres on how we process information. Our brains process words, images, spatial relationships and meanings in different parts of the brain. So, seeing a strategy on one page allows us to gather information simultaneously from a range of features of the diagram.

....
**In an increasingly complex business world,
a picture tells a thousand words.**
....

Converting your strategic plans into a visible project roadmap

Here's a step-by-step example of how you make your strategy visual. (I typically do this in person with a long roll of paper. Or I use an online collaboration tool such as Mural, Trello or Google Sheets.)

Here's how the process works:

1. You've got a strategy or plan.
2. You create the roadmap for a specific period – for example, 6, 12 or 24 months – and draw it up.
3. You draw on several horizontal 'lanes' to represent your business's key strategies or areas, such as 'customers', 'staff', and 'product development'.
4. You draw vertical lines to represent time intervals, such as one month or one quarter.
5. At the far right of each lane, you write down the 'arriving goal' you've agreed on. (Refer to the section 'The second hurdle: which measures?', earlier in this chapter.)
6. You ask each 'lane' leader to add the key projects they've already committed to, adding them as sticky notes or project cards on the roadmap.
7. You review the strategy and ask, 'What other projects do we need to add to hit the goals?'
8. You keep working on the map until it balances strategic ambition with business-as-usual reality.

The process is intuitive, and leadership teams I've worked with have taken to this process quickly.

Creating the roadmap leads to 'crunch' moments that make for high value discussions within the team. The kinds of issues that often emerge are discussed in the following sections.

The frontloading issue

There is a natural tendency to stack 80 per cent of the projects into the first half of the planning timeline. Visualising this on the roadmap often causes the team to pause – and may lead to long faces around the boardroom. It's an important reality check your team can solve using strategic sequencing (discussed later in this chapter).

The business-as-usual issue

I worked with one team that claimed to have 400 projects on their business-as-usual list before adding their contribution to the new company-wide strategy.

That might be extreme, but in this situation when you build the roadmap bottom-up (step 6 in the roadmap process), your team quickly realises they have their work cut out just keeping the trains running on time – before they even consider embracing big, bold strategic initiatives.

I often ask the leadership team to complete a quick activity at this point. I ask them to draw a triangle with three horizontal layers dividing it. Then I ask then to write 'Keeping the trains running' in the bottom layer, 'Making basic improvements' in the middle layer and 'Strategic leadership' in the top layer. Then I ask them to allocate a percentage of the team's total time in the last three months to each layer. Most commonly, it's something like 70 per cent, 25 per cent, 5 per cent.

We've established that unless something shifts, they have around 5 per cent of each individual's time – say two hours a week – to work on the big, bold strategic projects.

This is a sobering moment. But it leads to much more realistic plans, because they can still stretch to be ambitious, but they're stretching from a sensible starting point of how much time they have available.

The 'where-did-the-strategy-go?' issue

Often the first cut of a roadmap focuses on adding projects to the roadmap bottom-up – that is, the already known projects. Then, in step 7, your team adds a small number of projects necessary to make the transformation you need.

However, the transformational projects are outnumbered by all the business-as-usual projects, so the roadmap looks not much different to 'what we did last year'.

The crunch moment here is, 'Are we being ambitious enough?' This question can prompt the team to be braver with the translation of the strategy into specific projects.

For example, if the strategy revolves around entering a new market sector, is that easily visible across a range of critical projects on the roadmap?

To really focus on this area, one team I worked with chose to add a section on 'what's changing?' to their presentation of the strategy and roadmap to their wider team.

Cascading roadmaps

Suppose your whole-of-business strategy is divided into lanes such as Customers, People and Product. In that case, you will find it beneficial to have a functional leadership group take each lane and do a more detailed version for themselves.

For example, the HR team takes the People lane and divides it into three further lanes: Attract, Retain and Develop.

Or the Sales team takes the Customers lane, divides it up into Marketing, New Business and Retention, and then fleshes out the roadmap in more detail.

Once this is done, you'll likely find the People or Customer lanes' overall goals have changed based on their functional team's feedback, as will the roadmap.

This exercise is beneficial to gather feedback and strengthen the roadmap and strategy. And it also works to get buy-in from the functional teams.

Wrapping up the roadmap

Each of the issues we just walked through introduces a healthy debate and strengthens the strategy.

....

A strategy is nothing if it doesn't translate into a coherent calendar of real activity.

....

And the roadmap exercise gives the strategy a robust workout.

It's a great sign of the team's practical intelligence when they can turn their strategy into sticky goals and a visible project roadmap.

While many teams do plan to this level of detail – for example, in agile development – in my experience, it is rare in leadership teams.

And, therefore, this level of planning can give you competitive advantage because your plan is more likely to end up as reality. Your strategy is probably about as good as your competitor's in the boardroom on the other side of town. But your *execution* could be ten times better.

One final piece of the puzzle is needed to ensure the roadmap matches your ambition with the reality of your workload and resource limitations – strategic sequencing.

USING STRATEGIC SEQUENCING TO PRIORITISE YOUR PROJECTS

Strategy is making hard choices, and turning your strategy into a visible project roadmap can help surface – and resolve – these hard choices.

If you communicate these choices well, you may get your leadership team on the same page about what is most important. But it's not easy. In 'No one knows your strategy – not even your top leaders', Donald Sull, Charles Sull and James Yoder argue:

> Our analysis of 124 organizations revealed that only 28% of executives and middle managers responsible for executing strategy could list three of their company's strategic priorities.

To help you make and communicate these choices, I recommend a process I call strategic sequencing, shown in figure 9.3.

Strategic sequencing outlines how you and your leadership team can view the roadmap from four different perspectives in turn.

If you've set the roadmap up on a long piece of paper in your boardroom, I encourage you to walk around it and view it from some different angles.

Walk to the right side and take a look at the arriving goals. Will the current project roadmap get to you those goals? If not, why not? What's missing? This is the future-focused perspective.

Figure 9.3: Strategic sequencing: the four perspectives

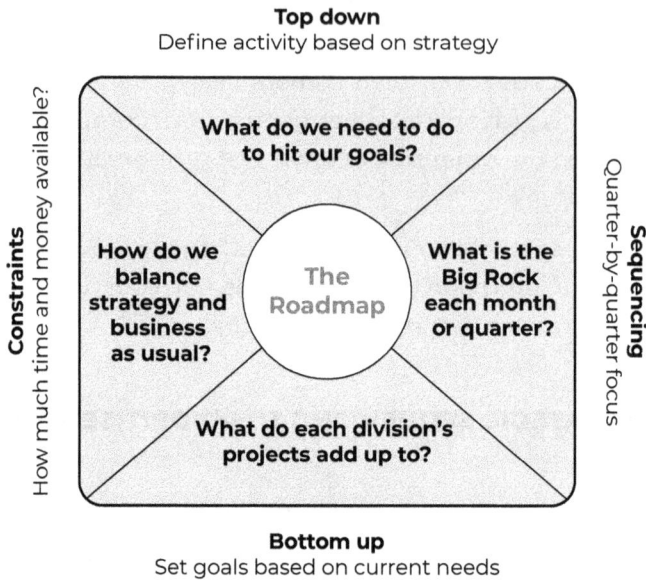

Top down
Define activity based on strategy

Constraints
How much time and money available?

What do we need to do
to hit our goals?

How do we
balance
strategy and
business
as usual?

The
Roadmap

What is the
Big Rock
each month
or quarter?

What do each division's
projects add up to?

Sequencing
Quarter-by-quarter focus

Bottom up
Set goals based on current needs

Standing in front of the roadmap, look at all the business-as-usual projects and ask, 'Does this meet the needs we have now, and does it connect to the team's day-to-day work?' This is the bottom-up perspective.

Answer the question from earlier in this chapter around the amount of time your teams have to spend on business-as-usual work versus strategic leadership. Then look at the roadmap to see if the goals and projects are realistic given the current time (and money) available. That's the constraints perspective.

Finally, take every single sticky note or card off the roadmap. Then, look at the first quarter and ask, 'What's the single most important project that quarter?' and put it back on the roadmap. I call this the 'big rock' project. Then ask, 'Which other projects are viable to run in that quarter too? Are there any which have synergy with the main one?' Then do the same for quarter two. Finally, go back to all the projects that didn't make it back on to the roadmap and either move them to a future period or decide whether you can eliminate or reduce them. That's the sequencing perspective.

I worked with a sales team who were overwhelmed when they built the roadmap bottom-up, and realised everything was stacked into quarter one. The team leader slumped in his chair. Then we went through the exercise of picking a 'big rock' project for each quarter. And the mood lifted and lifted until the team ended with a strategic roadmap that perfectly balanced ambition and reality. The shift in energy was palpable: the leader turned from slumped to pumped.

A further benefit to this sales lead was that his peers had said, 'We love the sales team, but you do release too many new initiatives that require everyone else to do considerable work. Can you slow down?' The big rocks also allowed his team to create a narrative to communicate a singular quarterly focus to the broader team.

Why strategic sequencing works

A little subtlety is required in this process. As the leader or member of the leadership team, you need to facilitate this process by taking the team on a tour of the four perspectives. As discussed in chapter 6, this approach is called a 'perspective tour'. It requires parallel thinking, and the whole team to consider the problem from each perspective simultaneously.

Often, the critical issue with prioritising is that people are coming from different perspectives. I'm thinking about which project is most important for my team who are suffering right now; you're thinking about which project gets you the maximum budget for new product development. Looking at the roadmap from the four perspectives of strategic sequencing resolves these conflicts.

I liken strategic sequencing's four perspectives to kneading dough. You roll the dough out, then turn it 90 degrees and knead it some more, before turning it another 90 degrees and so on. The different perspectives aren't divisive. Instead, they enable you to turn the roadmap around and look at it from different angles while keeping it in one piece.

If you do this well, your visible project roadmap now turns your goals into a motivating and realistic plan for your leadership team.

Now the real challenge begins: communicating this to the whole organisation, so everyone knows exactly what to do.

COMMUNICATE YOUR GOALS WITH THE 3 Es

When a leader looks at life through their wider team's eyes, they may get a surprise. What looks obvious and sensible to you looks incomprehensible – even crazy – when viewed from someone's perspective on the front line.

I remember many times as a middle manager when I was left scratching my head at the leadership team's decisions.

As I mention back in chapter 2, in one company I worked at, the newish CEO walked the senior managers through the new strategy, and I resolved to quit there and then. I remember describing it to a colleague as 'fixing yesterday's problems tomorrow'.

As fate would have it, I went back to my desk to find an email from a recruiter that gave me an exit path. I was gone 30 days later.

Let me be clear: I'm not saying I knew more than this well-known CEO and his leadership team. It's just that things look different when you're not across the whole business.

In 'The top complaints from employees about their leaders', Lou Solomon reports on research revealing employees' communication frustrations.

Employees called out the kind of management offences that point to a striking lack of emotional intelligence among business leaders, including micromanaging, bullying, narcissism, indecisiveness, and more.

To avoid these 'lost-in-translation' issues when you communicate your strategy, plan and goals, think about the three Es – explanation, expectation and empathy.

Explanation

Be as transparent as you can. Otherwise, decisions (such as firing their much-loved co-worker) can create misunderstandings and mistrust.

Employee engagement firm TINYpulse found the biggest driver of *employee happiness* is transparency – with a correlation of 0.93 between them, compared to only 0.35 between happiness and employee engagement.

Leadership teams often hesitate to communicate transparently for several reasons:

· We want to talk about a problem, but we don't have the answer yet.
· We want to talk about it, but it might worry some people.
· People don't need or want to know about it.

Each of these concerns may be valid in a particular instance, but this is when you need to draw on your principles and values and rely on your integrity and transparency to build employee trust and engagement for the long term. That also saves you having to make frequent decisions about what you can or should share.

Transparency isn't the only factor to consider in communicating your plans. You'll also want to share the appropriate level of detail. Most of your employees want the headlines plus the plan; they don't need to spend a long time going through a detailed rationale.

Working with one leadership team, we presented a draft strategy to their senior managers, and then I facilitated a private feedback session with them. They all said, 'Give me a little less time on the business rationale and a bit more time on the specific plans' – the roadmap. They want to know what it means for them in their area.

The leadership team overcame this by showing one slide in the presentation that highlighted some of the steps and analyses they'd worked through to arrive at the strategy. But the presentation didn't talk through the analysis in any detail. The result was strong buy-in from the senior managers who loved the headline explanations and detailed roadmap.

Expectation

Be clear and specific on what you expect people to do as a result of the decisions you've made.

The one-page strategy house (see chapter 13) and the visible project roadmap from earlier in this chapter create opportunities to show where each employee fits visually, and then explain what they need to be, what they need to do, or where they need to get to.

As internal communications expert Bill Quirke notes in *Making the Connections*:

> When employees understand their overall role in the business, 91% will work towards the organisation's success. But if they don't fully understand their role, that number plummets to 23%.

Empathy

Demonstrate you understand what it might look like from the employee's seat:

- How does this strategy or plan look if I'm in their role?
- What are they thinking and feeling at the moment?
- How do I want them to feel at the end of the presentation?

Remember, if you're communicating or presenting to someone, *they* are the hero of the presentation – not you. It rarely works to present as if you are the hero, even if you are the CEO.

I recommend starting with empathy, and connecting with the reality as they see it. For a client who was communicating a strategy to their team after a particular tough pandemic-hit year, we made sure they led the strategy presentation with a discussion of wins and losses from a tough year. We made sure they said, 'I see you' to the employees, not just, 'Here we go again for another year'.

Ensure the management team is aligned on these three Es, particularly the explanation, to avoid confusion. Build a culture of transparency to minimise politics, secrets and lies.

Chapter summary

To make your goals stick, get them out of your heads and into people's hands. To write powerful goals, pick your key results areas, and then support them using a combination of measurable arriving, doing and being goals.

The principles of excellent planning include creating a visible project roadmap, using strategic sequencing to solve prioritisation problems, and communicating your plans to the broader organisation with the 3 Es – empathy, explanation and expectation.

Take action

Make goals sticky and get them into people's hands through the following:

- Identify your key results areas: the parts of your business that you most need to measure and improve.
- Create measurable being, doing and arriving goals for each key result area.
- Draw up a visible project roadmap.
- Use strategic sequencing to make the roadmap realistically ambitious.
- Communicate the plan with the 3 Es: empathy, explanation, expectation.

That's the initial launch of your strategic plans taken care of. You're off to a great start.

And to make sure your goals make an impact, you'll need to consistently remind your wider team of the goals – and encourage their direct managers to coach employees through any challenges.

Next

Once your goals are defined and communicated, you still need to track progress and conduct post-analysis – the topics of the next two chapters. These are two areas where leadership teams often have room for improvement.

10

Progress.
Tracking progress and changing course.

LOST IN THE DESERT

Could you walk in a straight line if you were set down in the Sahara Desert?

In 2009, four researchers sent people to the Sahara and asked them to walk in a straight line for several hours. They also conducted the same experiment in a forest, outlining their findings in 'Walking straight into circles', published in *Current Biology*. (JL Souman, et al.)

The researchers found that if the walkers could see the sun or moon, they could walk in a more-or-less straight line.

But if the sun was behind clouds, or the moon had not risen, participants walked in circles, sometimes crossing their previous path several times without noticing.

In some instances, the circles walked were as small as 20 metres in diameter. And yet the walkers were trying their best, and expending considerable energy, to keep moving in a consistent direction.

If you want to make progress, you need to have a reference point to check against regularly.

And if you don't keep an eye on the sky, the big picture, then your team may go round in circles, cover the same ground, and ultimately get nowhere.

Learning from this metaphor, let's explore the three aspects of making progress:

1. *Track progress:* Work out where you are relative to your destination, and your projected roadmap.
2. *Communicate progress:* Tell everyone where the organisation is, and how it's tracking.
3. *Change course:* Make adjustments to keep you on track.

In my 2020 research surveying 30 leadership teams, I identified a drop-off from their ratings for *planning* behaviours to their ratings for *progress* behaviours. Leadership teams seem to lose some focus after making a plan, and sometimes fail to follow up and track their progress.

In this chapter, I outline simple ways to stay on track.

TRACKING PROGRESS

People walking through the desert are a far cry from leaders running a business. Let's switch to another metaphor, which will help us explore how companies can track progress: the pilot on the flight deck.

To safely fly from Sydney to Singapore, the pilot uses:

· detailed coordinates for the destination
· a detailed flight path with key checkpoints
· enough fuel to get to the destination
· multiple instruments to check the aeroplane's path
· dashboards to communicate the information to the pilot
· an autopilot system to do the easy steering
· a co-pilot to check and challenge the pilot.

In the previous chapter, you saw how to make sticky goals and a visible roadmap. These connect with the first two points in the preceding list.

We also looked at strategic sequencing – making sure the roadmap is realistic, given the resources available. That's the third point.

How do we address the fourth and fifth points: to create the systems and dashboards to track progress? How do we make sure your business isn't flying, or walking, around in circles?

The strategic business dashboard

Most business dashboards are operational: they focus on the current performance of the business. Typically, the list of metrics on a dashboard includes:

- finances
- customers
- sales and marketing
- processes
- staff.

You can choose the appropriate performance metrics for your dashboard by considering these questions:

- Who's using the dashboard, and how will they use it?
- Do you have a comprehensive set of metrics for the critical aspects of business performance?
- Is the dashboard easy to understand and hard to misunderstand?
- Are the metrics given context – for example, a comparison with a prior period, a moving average, or industry benchmarks?

And for each of your chosen performance metrics, you can try to use real-time or near-real-time data in the dashboard – and show how the metrics are changing over time.

However, these performance metrics can be hard to turn into course-adjustments because they may not reveal a problem, let alone the cause of any problem.

Other metrics might get you closer to understanding your progress, not just your performance.

Pacing metrics

To create a business dashboard that tracks progress, not just performance, you may want to add pacing metrics.

When I worked in a large sales team, we knew that to hit our quarterly sales target of $25 million, we had to be at 40 per cent of target – $10 million – going into the first day of the quarter. In other words, we had to sell 40 per cent before the quarter started. We also had pacing numbers like this for each week. And depending on the numbers, we could adjust the sales strategy accordingly.

Pacing metrics are useful for arriving goals but can also be used for doing goals. (Refer to the previous chapter for more on these types of goals.)

Project metrics

Project metrics are about measuring the critical projects needed to transform the business and hit your plans. Is the new finance system roll out on track? Has the brand refresh been finished?

Project metrics capture the doing goals and are easiest for the wider team to be accountable to.

Pattern metrics

If you are tracking projects, performance and pacing, you can understand whether you are making enough progress.

You might also want to dig into one more level. The *pattern* metric indicates how much you are learning from the other metrics – what patterns have you learnt? And it can measure how well you are adjusting your strategy.

The best way to capture these is to keep a decision register as part of the dashboard, which details all the major course adjustments you've made, whether they worked and what you learnt. That way, the dashboard becomes a living document, not just a moment in time.

Matt Mullenweg, the co-founder of WordPress and CEO of Automattic, has been recording the decisions of his company for the last 15 years. Talking with Shane Parrish on the *Knowledge Project* podcast, he says this searchable register of the thinking behind the decisions is the most valuable asset of his business.

You can see how the four dashboard elements of performance, pacing, projects and patterns come together in figure 10.1.

Figure 10.1: The four elements in a strategic dashboard

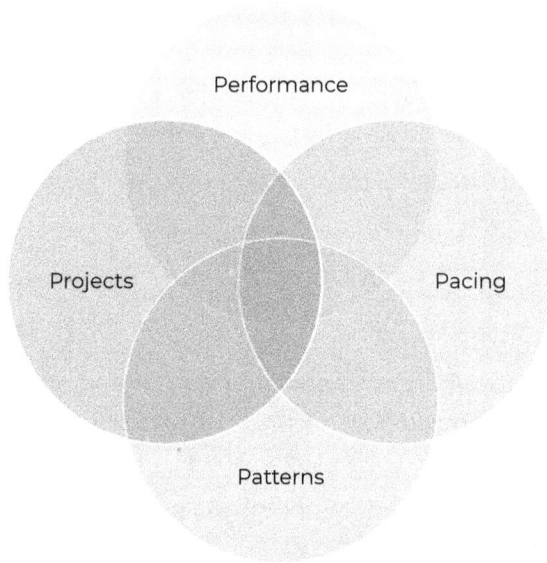

Performance

Projects

Pacing

Patterns

Figure 10.1 shows how the typical operational or performance metrics remain at the top, but can be supplemented by projects, pacing and patterns. In our aeroplane analogy, this dashboard doesn't just show the engine's performance, but also tells you how far you have left to travel and whether you're on track (pacing), along with what you need to do next (projects) and how quickly you're learning.

Perhaps you've tried to build a dashboard before and found your data was too slow, or people didn't use it, or the metrics were too variable. In other words, people didn't trust the dashboard.

....

Having a range of performance data plus pacing, projects and patterns can bolster your dashboard because it will become more strategic, and not just operationally focused.

....

It will help you not only measure progress but also better understand the business you work in. What works, what doesn't, what parts of the business affect other parts?

A dashboard example

Figure 10.2 shows an example of how a strategic dashboard could look.

Figure 10.2 includes the following elements:

- *Performance* is represented by the goals you set. (Refer to chapter 9 for more on this.)
- *Projects* can be represented using a traffic light system – green is on track, amber indicates some concerns, while red signals significant problems – so the leadership team knows which ones to pay attention to. In the example, they are rated on impact (are they set to deliver), confidence (how likely is the rest of the project to be delivered?), and ease (any significant problems or roadblocks?). These are the three ICE criteria to choose between projects, outlined in chapter 8.
- *Pacing* can be used for goals achieved across the year. Sales revenue is an excellent pacing metric. Goals that may happen at a specific time or aren't easy to measure regularly should not be used as pacing metrics. For example, if you only measure staff engagement once or twice a year, it will not make a useful pacing metric.
- *Patterns* can be used to record what you're learning. You may be learning in three ways:
  1. from your regular pit stops (see chapter 11), where you take time out to reflect and refuel as a team
  2. from your pivots, where you have changed course reacting to internal or external data (see the section 'Changing course', later in this chapter)
  3. from your experiments, where you deliberate tried some-thing new (refer to chapter 8).

The dashboard can be as simple or as complex as you need. But when it comes to communicating progress to the wider team, you'll want to have a simple version to explain what's happening, and clarify your expectations of people moving forward.

Figure 10.2: An example strategic dashboard

Performance

1. People	2. Product	3. Partners	4. Process	5. Profile	6. Profit
People goal: How do you need skill, motivation and consistent behaviours to improve?	Product goal: how is the number or quality of products and services improving?	Partner goal: how are customers getting more value and staying longer?	Process goal: how can you deliver more value to customers, more consistently, with less overall effort?	Profile goal: how well is your marketing working to acquire customers, and build your brand?	As a result what sustainable profit will you earn?
Engagement | Culture | Skill	Quality | Production | Innovation	Satisfaction | Loyalty | NPS	Value creation | Compliance	Brand health | Acquisition	Revenue | Costs | Margin

Pacing

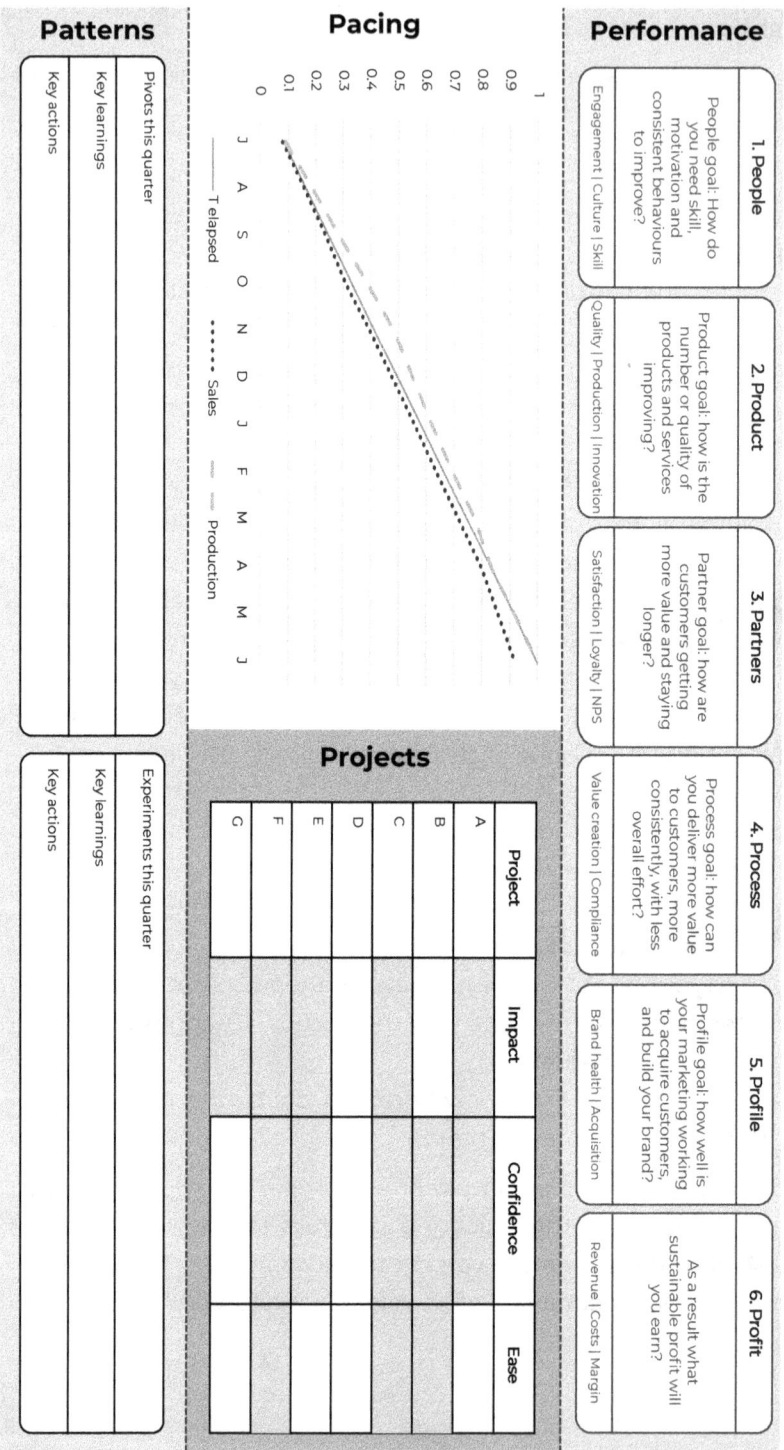

Vertical axis: 1, 0.9, 0.8, 0.7, 0.6, 0.5, 0.4, 0.3, 0.2, 0.1, 0

Horizontal axis: J A S O N D J F M A M J

Legend: —— T elapsed ······ Sales —— Production

Projects

Project	Impact	Confidence	Ease
A			
B			
C			
D			
E			
F			
G			

Patterns

Pivots this quarter	Experiments this quarter
Key learnings	Key learnings
Key actions	Key actions

Communication problems

Sydney, 2018. I'm running a workshop on goal setting for senior managers in a mid-size organisation. We start talking about the connection of their goals to the overall organisation's strategy. The conversation went a little like this:

> Me: 'How familiar are you with the company strategy?'
>
> Alex, turns to his colleagues: 'Is the strategy the iceberg-diagram-thingy they presented mid-year?'
>
> Hayley: 'No, it was that document presented at the town hall in December.'
>
> Alex: 'Right. So where can we get a copy of that?'
>
> Fiona: 'I think it's saved in the G Drive under Management Team.'
>
> Hayley: 'I don't even have access to the G Drive.'

How likely is it that this group of senior, well-paid, managers can translate the leadership team's strategic plans into reality?

COMMUNICATING PROGRESS

Only 9 per cent of employees agree they 'know what's happening most of the time' according to a 2012 study by the American Management Association.

Lack of communication is one of the most common complaints employees make about their leaders.

And according to the Economist Intelligence Unit's 2018 report *Communication Barriers in the Modern Workplace*:

> Poor communication is having a tremendous impact on the workplace. Unclear instructions from superiors, pointless meetings and other stressors can snowball into larger issues with widespread impacts on the business. Respondents say communication barriers are leading to a delay or failure to complete projects (44 per cent), low morale (31 per cent), missed performance goals (25 per cent) and even lost sales (18 per cent) – some worth hundreds of thousands of dollars.

In my experience, leadership teams vastly underestimate the quantity and quality of communication required to get their wider team fully 'bought-in' to the strategy and able to translate the words and ideas into their daily work of managing teams and projects.

In general, leadership teams know they need to tell their wider team about the strategy or plan in some kind of kick-off meeting. (For more in this area, see my tips on communicating the plan in chapter 9.) But they underestimate the consistency and repetition required on an ongoing basis.

You could think of this communication process a bit like a marketing campaign. You are marketing your plan to the team in order to change their behaviour – similar to a marketer trying to launch a new line of shampoo.

You need to drive top-of-mind awareness through the frequency of communicating the plan.

You need to make sure people understand your message – it must be simple and show them how they fit in and what they need to do.

You need to communicate in a way that they are motivated by your message – how will it make their life easier or better?

And you need to make it easy for them to change their behaviour by reminding them near the point of purchase – as they head into a team meeting, say.

This process involves a lot more than just running a kick-off meeting and emailing a plan. It needs layers of different types of communication. Otherwise, they are going to keep using the shampoo they've always used, and your shampoo (your new plan) will gather dust.

Communication benefits

....
Communicating progress is about reinforcing your plan, deepening understanding, maximising motivation, and minimising barriers.
....

Your functional teams benefit from you communicating progress regularly. They are more connected to the strategy. They feel their role is more important. They judge their leaders as transparent, which makes them happier. And they no longer need to complain in surveys that 'I never know what's going on'.

More than that though, the leadership team benefits in these ways:

- You are far more likely to achieve your goals, because they stay top-of-mind. McKinsey's 2015 survey 'How to beat the transformation odds' suggested when the leadership team 'communicated openly and across the organisation about the transformation's progress and success' the transformation in question was eight times more likely to succeed in the long term.
- Your culture will be more positive, because people see where they fit in and how they can contribute.
- Staff retention will be higher, because people feel like they are making progress and working for an excellent leadership team.

And that's not all. Communicating progress is a two-way street – so the process gives you a critical opportunity to ask questions, explore blockers and receive qualitative frontline feedback on how plans and projects are progressing.

Many experts argue that a critical role for organisations is to learn – see, for example, Peter Senge's *The Fifth Discipline* or Amy Edmondson's *Teaming*. Communicating with your team about progress allows you to create this learning opportunity, through having a two-way dialogue about all elements of your dashboard:

- projects
- pacing
- performance
- patterns.

The communication plan

Suppose you treat the communication of your plan and your progress like a multimedia marketing campaign. In that case, you may want to dial up the frequency, while mixing up the communication channels.

**Increase the frequency and coverage of your communication.
Every week. Every leader. Every channel.**

....

Can you make sure people are reminded of the plan and progress every week? This does not need to be simple repetition. It could shift focus between data, real stories, celebrating wins and project milestones.

Can you make sure the communication doesn't only come from one person? Your leadership team and wider group of leaders should be able to keep the conversation going in their team meetings and corridor conversations.

Can you mix up the channels, so your ongoing communication features town-hall-style meetings, update emails, lunch-with-the-leader meetings, and visible dashboards on the wall?

Revisiting the 3Es

In the previous chapter, I discussed the three Es for leadership communication: empathy, explanation and expectation.

When it comes to designing the content and delivery of your progress updates, you may need to dial up the first E, empathy, to make sure the updates are interactive and two-way.

You'll want to explain the data (if you're presenting data), so people understand what you're trying to say. And you'll want to spell out your expectations – what needs to be done differently from here.

The leadership team as role models

The leadership team must also role-model the behaviours being asked from others, and the focus on the key projects and performance outcomes.

....

**Communication is just as much about
what you do, as what you say.**

....

A sobering statistic from McKinsey's 'How to beat the transformation odds', was that '33 per cent of failed transformations occur because the leadership team's behaviours did not support the desired changes'.

In the same research, they saw a 5.3 times greater likelihood of a successful transformation project if leaders role-modelled the behaviours they were asking employees to make.

One organisation I worked with was pushing their wider team to adopt a new system for internal communication while four of the leaders refused to use it. They turned to me for help with change management, and I said I wouldn't run any sessions with the wider team until the leadership team were aligned.

Your leadership team should have an explicit discussion, and make firm agreements on the leadership behaviours you need to role-model to support your plans.

Communicating progress requires role modelling, a communication plan and two-way communications. It requires consistent effort from the leadership team, but the benefits are numerous. Without these factors, your plans and transformation projects have a negligible chance of success.

Take action

To communicate progress, work with your leadership team on a robust two-way communication plan. Put your marketing hats on to treat it like an internal marketing plan, not just a progress update.

One leadership team I work with has built their weekly team meetings around their four key strategic pillars. The agenda runs through People, Product, Partners and Profit and allows for discussion and progress tracking. It's a simple approach, but it makes sure the link from annual strategy to weekly focus is clearly and frequently communicated.

CHANGING COURSE

With a bit of training, flying a plane from Sydney to Singapore becomes routine and predictable.

Business projects and strategies are a different game. The leadership team may not have a clear destination (they might know roughly where they're going, instead of exactly). They might not know if they have enough resources to get there. They don't know which competitors might beat them to it.

So to discuss changing course, let's also switch metaphors – because monitoring the progress of your strategic plans and projects is more like a game of poker than a point-to-point flight.

Poker is a game of limited information and significant uncertainty.

If we take the most common version, Texas hold 'em, each player is dealt two cards face-down so that only they can have a look at them. Three cards are then dealt face-up into the middle of the table for everyone to see followed by a fourth card and a fifth card, with rounds of betting after each.

Players bet money based on the best five-card hand their hidden cards can make when combined with any three or four of the five face-up cards.

If you have a king and a seven in your hand, for example, and on the table are ace, king, ten, six and two, then you have a pair of kings which is not a bad hand; however, it would be beaten if another player has an ace in their hand.

The parallels for business include:

- Some information is commonly available, while some is available to each player exclusively.
- As the hand progresses, you can see a little more information unfolding.
- At any point, you can choose to check (keep playing, without raising the stakes), raise (put more resources against the project) or fold (quit the project and save your chips for the next hand).

Projects are bets

Treating projects as bets leads to a subtle, but significant, shift in mindset.

Instead of treating projects as set-in-stone must-wins, you can see them as one of a series of bets you're making to try to get ahead and hit your goals.

Instead of believing these projects are guaranteed to deliver the desired result, you can think of them as percentage plays, and be a little less attached.

Music-streaming leader Spotify has used a process they call DIBB – Data, Insight, Belief, Bet – to deliver critical innovations.

An example quoted by agile coach Henrik Kniberg is how Spotify handled users' transition from desktop to mobile:

- They saw the *data* – the percentage of mobile users rapidly climbing.
- That led to an *insight* – mobile would soon overtake desktop usage, and they had very few developers skilled in mobile.
- That led to a *belief* – for long-term survival, we need to start thinking mobile-first.
- And the result was that they placed some *bets* – on hiring mobile developers, training some desktop developers, and building the infrastructure for mobile development.

Once a bet – basically a strategic initiative, and an allocation of resource – is placed, the bet can be monitored, tracked and adjusted based on incoming data.

This new data can appear from two sources:

1. *Internal* data is exclusive data to you, and it helps you ascertain your likelihood of success. If the project deadlines are being missed or the project's impact is less than envisioned, your hand is becoming weaker. In the poker analogy, this is like thinking you had a king–seven and then on looking again, it's more like a jack–three.
2. *External* data is publicly available and helps you assess how other players are doing. This might be market conditions, customer data and economic indicators. In poker, these are the face-up cards.

Any time you review a project's progress, you can choose to check, raise or fold based on the changes in the external and internal data.

A summary of your options is shown in figure 10.3.

You can choose to re-assess the odds on each bet at regular intervals – say, every two or four weeks. Between these reviews, you remain 100 per cent committed to doing the work. And then at the review point, you enter into an objective analysis of new data and decide whether to check, raise or fold.

Bet combinations

You will, no doubt, have multiple projects and plans running simultaneously.

As mentioned, Spotify is a believer in treating their projects and critical decisions as bets. As a result, they have a 'bet board' showing all the bets they are currently playing and future bets they want to make.

Figure 10.3: Tracking internal and external conditions to decide whether to bet, check or fold

		Internal conditions (progress)		
		Worse	Same	Better
External conditions (progress)	Better for you	Check	Bet	Bet
	Same for you	Check or Fold	Check	Bet
	Worse for you	Fold	Check or Fold	Check

Likewise, you can take a six-month period on your project roadmap and consider each project as a bet you're placing. Each bet is in the format: if we do *x* series of actions, we predict we will get *y* result.

Knowing when to fold

When pursuing a strategic goal or the completion of a project, you've no doubt been taught that resilience is essential. In practice, most projects don't get completed, let alone become sustainable successes.

Many projects grind to a halt without anyone making a decision to stop. They slow down. People stop talking about them. They languish on a project list. Resources are re-allocated.

Instead, it is better to make 'go/no-go' decisions at critical junctures by reviewing the internal and external data and deciding whether to continue.

Projects often get stopped too early – or go on too long. Two cognitive biases can lead to these non-optimal decisions (and waste of your scarce resources).

The valley of despair

The 'valley of despair', a concept from James Clear's *Atomic Habits*, denotes the gap between how quickly we think we'll see the benefits of our work, compared to how quickly those benefits accrue in real life.

In projects, a lag nearly always exists between doing the work and getting the result. We often fall prey to the planning fallacy – where we underestimate the time and effort required to deliver a project and overestimate the benefit from that project.

The valley of despair makes us feel like giving up. We had expected to get immediate advantages from our project, yet we are working harder than we thought and things don't seem to be shifting.

This can easily lead people to start slowing down and thinking about another shiny new project they could be doing instead; a silver bullet that will change everything.

The time lag of the valley of despair has killed many projects that might have gone on to be beneficial, if the project owners had had the disciplined thought and disciplined action of Jim Collins (author of *Good to Great*, among others). When describing the conditions necessary to drive change, he uses the metaphor of the 'flywheel': it can take tremendous effort to get a flywheel going, but it can gather impressive momentum when it does. Disciplined thought and disciplined action are two of his tactics to start gathering momentum.

The sunk cost effect

A well-known cognitive bias that moves us in the opposite direction from abandoning a project too soon is the 'sunk cost effect'.

If you see someone lose $500 at the casino and then keep betting to win back their money, you could see this as chasing sunk costs. You can never get that particular $500 back, so any new bets should be made without considering the sunk $500.

With projects, you and your leadership team may feel that when you have come so far – gone through scores of meetings, significant capital investment and months of time – then even though the results seem to be below par, you need to keep on going. You can have the explicit idea that you've come this far, so you have to follow through.

Making a balanced decision to fold, or not

How should leadership teams balance these biases?

First, be less attached to your projects. They are a means to an end, not an end in themselves.

Second, consider them as bets and estimate the changing probability that they will get the result you want. Use the internal and external changing data to guide you.

Third, run experiments or tests (where possible) to assess whether 'action *x* gets result *y*' while investing considerably less time and money.

Knowing when to check

In poker, a 'check' is when a player taps their finger on the table to indicate, 'I am happy to stay in and see some more cards dealt face-up, as long as no-one else raises the stakes'.

In the business world, a check is saying, 'Let's keep going on this project and wait for some more data'. This will be the action you take most often, when you're intending to complete projects and 'do what we said we'd do'.

However, checking has a real cost: the time, money and effort your team puts into this project, and the burn rate of cash involved in the project. Keeping bets in play in the real world costs money. Therefore, you may want to understand the resources being burnt up by the project per week before deciding to stay in the hand for a few more weeks.

What is your opportunity cost? Could you cut-and-run and invest those same resources in a better project? Or should you work through the valley of despair and see if you can find the start of the upward shift and the beginning of momentum?

Knowing when to raise

Projects usually have a fixed budget (if they have a budget at all; many less formal projects don't).

Sometimes you may be asked to add more funds to the budget to get the same (or less) outcome as initially promised.

And sometimes you may see a project deliver better-than-expected results.

In these instances, if you treat your projects as bets, you can make an impartial decision on further investment.

If your position improves based on internal data, you may choose to up your investment to improve the outcomes or delivery speed.

If your position has weakened (for example, internal data shows you underestimated the required budget), you will be more likely to consider folding or checking before you potentially throw good money after bad.

But it's not a game

One of the limitations of the poker analogy is that poker is a zero-sum game. If I win, you lose. At the end of the night, precisely the same amount of money is divided among all the players (unless you play in a casino, where the house takes a percentage and so you're playing a negative-sum game).

Business, however, can be a positive-sum game where multiple parties can win. By creating more value for consumers, they can grow the size of the whole market.

You can even see business as an 'infinite game' (see, for example, James P Carse's *Finite and Infinite Games* and Simon Sinek's *The Infinite Game*), where the rules aren't obvious, the competitive set is ill-defined, and you often play to be a better version of yourself.

This implies that you and your leadership team should rely more on internal data than data about competitors when judging your bets. You can still check with customers to see if they see an improvement, you can check economic indicators to see if your pricing model is appropriate, and you can check project delivery times. But you may pay less attention to the press releases from a competitor spruiking how well their new shiny product or service is going. They are probably bluffing or, at the very least, exaggerating the strength of their hand.

Chapter summary

Every plan will go off course, but not every planner will know *how far* off course they are, or how to get back on track. Tracking progress consists of designing a dashboard, communicating progress (listening and sharing) and changing course when necessary.

When you've made plans and tracked progress, how do you decide whether to change course? This chapter explored the poker metaphor and offered a grid to help you decide whether to check, raise or fold, based on new external and internal data.

Take action

Track progress, communicate progress and change course as needed with the following:

- Build a strategic dashboard that shows performance, pacing, projects and patterns.
- Conduct regular reviews, every two to four weeks, of critical projects, between which times you stay 100 per cent committed to doing the work.
- When you're communicating strategies and plans to your wider organisation, treat it like a marketing campaign. You need to raise awareness of the plan, increase consideration or buy-in, and drive behavioural change.
- Together with your leadership team, make unbiased assessments of project progress, and clear-eyed decisions on when to fold and allocate resources elsewhere.
- Above all, try to avoid projects drifting slowly into the twilight zone where they are still chewing up resources but with no realistic prospect of achieving their original goals.

Next

In the next chapter, I outline how to gain greater understanding from your wins and losses by taking time out to look back and learn.

11

Pit stops.
Take regular time to reflect and refuel.

FAILING TO LEARN

Here's the outline of a conversation from a leadership team offsite.

Alex (CEO): 'One of the things we have to get better at is converting the new business opportunities that come our way. We should have won the tender last month for Ripco Retail. We had been building the relationship for 12 months. We were in pole position.'

Carla (GM): 'It still hurts. I can't believe we lost. We even know the competitor who won, and we know what they would have said. We know we are better than them.'

Facilitator: 'Have you taken the time to review the tender process and see what you can do differently?'

Alex: 'No, we haven't managed to review it yet. But our new business strategy has to be the number one priority for next year.'

Alex and Carla's business is – by their own reckoning – not making as much progress as they'd like. They don't take time to squeeze the learnings out of their successes and failures. Instead, they keep moving onwards to the next project. Are they really moving onwards if they don't take time to learn? Or are they more like someone having a tennis lesson who keeps having tennis balls fired at them – and keeps making the same mistakes?

In a conversation about accountability, another leader lamented to me, 'I don't mind if my team makes mistakes, but we keep making the same ones.' I asked him if his team assigned a specific time to take stock of their projects, and he said, 'Sometimes. We are getting a little better at it on big projects.'

···················

Remember – the leadership team's intelligence comes from a process of collective learning.

···················

In *Teaming*, Amy Edmondson outlines six principles for collective learning. Teams need to:

- ask questions
- share information
- seek help
- experiment with unproven actions
- talk about mistakes
- seek feedback.

These principles are brought to life in leadership teams when they have full and frank conversations about their work in three time-scales: the future, the present and the past.

The object of this collective learning is to gather more information, deepen the leadership team's understanding and improve its capabilities.

This chapter outlines how your leadership team can get these benefits by conducting regular reviews – what I call 'pit stops'.

The name came from a client of mine, David Roddick, who takes his leadership team offsite for a whole day each quarter to focus on the big picture: to review strategy, to learn as a team and to build relationships.

Pit stops have a specific structure that differentiates them from typical project reviews. Project reviews may be held every two or four weeks and use dashboards to review key elements. Pit stops, on the other hand, allow your leadership team to take more time to review bigger picture issues.

Typically, a quarterly pit stop might revolve around the leadership team considering the following questions:

- *The EQ (emotional intelligence) question:* How are our working relationships?
- *The PQ (practical intelligence) question:* Are our delivery and project systems supporting the execution of strategy?
- *The IQ (creative-analytical intelligence) question:* Can we strengthen our strategy?

Let's review the general principles of conducting a pit stop to ensure the leadership team learns and implements improvements. And then you can start to tackle these three questions.

LOOKING BACK INSTEAD OF LOOKING DOWN

In my early twenties, I hitchhiked from Nairobi to Cape Town, and one of the places I visited was the Chimanimani Mountains in south-east Zimbabwe. Along with a group of international backpackers, we embarked on a three-day trek through challenging terrain.

I recall realising on day two that I was spending so much time looking at the ground in front of me – to avoid tripping on the rocky paths – that I was forgetting to appreciate the scenery.

This focus on the immediate next step, and avoiding tripping over, reminds me of what most of us do at work. Instead, we should spend more time looking further ahead. And some time looking backwards to where we just came from.

....

Looking back is a chance to learn – but most leadership teams keep relentlessly focused on what's immediately in front of them.

....

In 2012, researchers Scott Tannenbaum and Christopher Cerasoli set out to discover if after-action reviews, a standard part of leadership in the military, were effective in the corporate world.

(I have a particular affinity for this topic. When I was growing up, my family would pay the card game Bridge. I liked to discuss the play of each hand afterwards, while my family always wanted to move on to the next hand.)

Tannenbaum and Cerasoli's paper 'Do team and individual debriefs enhance performance? A meta-analysis,' came up with a clear answer – and a caveat.

....
Effective after-action reviews can deliver a 25 per cent effectiveness boost to teams.
....

Let's just pause to absorb this. We spend our lives as leaders eking out incremental 1 per cent gains, and yet here is an opportunity for a 25 per cent improvement that simply involves reviewing the work we've already done!

The caveat? You need to structure your reviews in specific ways. Before discussing the principles to keep in mind when structuring your reviews, let's spend a little more time on why these reviews are so important.

The importance of post-analysis to learn from your wins and losses

In his influential book *The Fifth Discipline*, Peter Senge argues that the primary function of organisations is to learn, and that the central unit of learning is the team. If individuals learn something new, it may be of some use to the organisation. But if a team goes through a learning process, the learning can be adopted much more widely.

If we stop for a moment to consider how teams learn, we can create a simplified model.

....
Intention > Action > Reaction > Discussion > Evolution
....

You form an intention, you take action, it has consequences, and you then discuss the outcomes to discover the key learnings you can use to improve performance in the next piece of work.

It's safe to say most leaders know these after-action reviews and discussions are a worthy endeavour. And I'd estimate most leadership teams conduct reviews – sometimes. But, in all the leadership team workshops and offsites I've been engaged on, only one leader I work with always includes a look-back-and-learn section in his brief to me.

In fact, in my 2020 survey of 30 leadership teams, I asked people how much of a strength the following statement was, 'We conduct post-mortems on our work and projects to learn from our wins and losses.' The average rating, out of 5, was 2.59. Of all the statements included in my Team Intelligence Diagnostic, this one rates consistently at, or near, the bottom.

Leaders know reviews are important, and they admit actually doing them is not a strength. What's causing this discrepancy?

The best way to answer this is to look back and learn, and work with your leadership team to answer the question: Why don't *we* conduct as many after-action reviews as we should? To do that review, let's first explore the structure of an after-action review, and then apply it.

Five principles for structuring an after-action review

In 'Do team and individual debriefs enhance performance?', Tannenbaum and Cerasoli have gifted us a comprehensive meta-analysis of after-action reviews, including testing ideas about their structure. That provides a platform to build an effective process for leadership teams to use.

The role of the leader is critical. You'll do well to create the right environment of psychological safety and make sure the discussion is structured.

Where possible, you'll do even better if you engage a neutral or external facilitator – Tannenbaum and Cerasoli found that an external facilitator increased the effectiveness gain for the team from 25 per cent to 38 per cent.

I've built on their findings using my experience with leadership teams and created five principles, under the acronym RAISE.

Regular

After-action reviews are not something you do once a year; they should be conducted during and after any significant project. But they don't need to be lengthy – the average length in the study was 18 minutes.

One practice I adopted when I was Chief Strategy Officer was to review important presentations in the taxi on the way back from the client's office. I found it an excellent place to conduct a post-mortem on the presentation, and to give and receive feedback with my team.

Active

This is a lean-in dialogue with your team members. It's not a debate or a competition of ideas. It's a search for the truth. Ask team members to add their perspectives together until you gain a clear picture of what happened and why.

Inclusive

Leaders must create an atmosphere of psychological safety (see Amy Edmondson's work) to allow for learning. After-action reviews need to be safe spaces where people can offer their perspective without fear of being judged. The leader does not do all the talking – instead, the leader facilitates a discussion that is free of blame and full of learning opportunities.

Structure

Use four questions to structure the review:

1. *Intention:* What was our intention? It's a critical piece of the discussion – you need to go back to your initial goals. Don't just review results from a position of hindsight.
2. *Actuality:* What actually happened? Get the facts – how did it play out compared to your goals and plans? What were the outcomes?
3. *Cause:* What caused the difference? Look for the causal factors, the new connections you need to make. These will help you better understand how your business works.
4. *Take-away:* What's the take-away? How can we immediately apply what we learnt?

Executional

For the after-action review to lead to a gain in effectiveness, the learnings need to be immediately integrated into an upcoming project. It's no use creating a review document, or making vague intentions to do things differently next time. You must find a way, right now, to use what you learnt. What live projects are you working on that can benefit from your learnings?

Why leadership teams don't look back and learn

Using the four Structure questions, let's examine why leaders neglect the after-action review.

My working hypothesis is that everyone has completed a proper project post-analysis in the past, but they didn't find them compelling and useful enough to build a regular practice with their team. In short, their previous post-mortems weren't helpful. Why?

Intentions

To complete after-action reviews, you need to have started a specific project with clear intentions. Let's say you were completing a tender for a new piece of business and you didn't win. Did you have clear intentions at the start of the tender for precisely what you were trying to do differently this time? Without being able to look back at clear, documented goals, after-action reviews are much less effective.

Actuality

Answering 'What actually happened?' requires some level of facts. Often the impact of a piece of work is not realised until some way into the future, so a time lag occurs between remembering 'why we did what we did' and seeing the outcomes.

Causation

Humans naturally look for cause and effect relationships (refer to chapter 6). Often, these tend to be singular and simplistic: 'We lost the tender because our competitor offered lower prices'. In chapter 6, I discussed going deeper, and explored ways to conduct a more thorough cause and effect analysis, enumerating the different parts of the system, and how they may affect each other.

Takeaways

The takeaways from reviews can often be too vague, have no immediate action or no owner. Perhaps your review meetings end with a 'must try better next time' or 'we need to be more competitive on price'. Instead, you and your leadership team can be focused on how you can tweak similar future projects based on what you learnt and what immediate steps you can put in place.

Leadership teams exist in a world that prioritises action, not retrospection. The focus is on immediate actions and long-term strategy. Taking time to look back and learn is not top-of-the-list when it comes to leadership team meetings.

And this is especially so when after-action reviews that do occur lack structure, have unclear outcomes, and may even turn into finger-pointing and blame games.

After-action reviews are a general idea that may be applied to any project. Leadership teams also have an opportunity to schedule quarterly reviews – pit stops – that encourage the team to take a 'bigger picture' perspective on the last quarter and all its learnings. The pit stop can focus on three key questions, discussed in the following sections.

PIT STOP QUESTION 1: EQ AND RELATIONSHIPS

As introduced earlier in this chapter, the Emotional Intelligence (EQ) question is, 'How are our working relationships?'

Building empathy

In late 2020, the head of sales for a large organisation in Melbourne asked me to help her with a planning day. She had a large leadership team with ten members, and they were set to spend a day on planning the next year.

The organisation had endured a particularly tough year, with COVID-19 blowing a hole in their revenue. As a result, they had spent the year fighting fires. Not only that, but they had been unable to replace key staff due to the challenging financial situation.

I suggested the possibility of spending the first hour reviewing the past year, to give the team a chance to breathe and connect before running headlong into the next 12 months.

In the end, this discussion at the start of the day was 'a game-changer' in her words. We asked each member of the leadership team to write down their high points, low points and turning points of 2020, and then discuss them with two others. We then had a whole-team conversation about the themes that emerged.

The leadership team got to deeply listen to their teammates' experiences of COVID- and lockdown-induced crises – both their work experiences and everyone's personal challenges. (Also in late 2020, I asked another room of leaders, 'Who had a personal challenge this year?' and every hand went up.)

The high-points/low-points conversation helps build empathy in the team. It also helps all members realise the benefits of being part of a team (often the highpoints are team-related). They also start to appreciate some of the fantastic work the team did, which invariably passed by without time to stop and celebrate.

And they can then turn their attention outwards and ask, 'How do we think our wider team are feeling now? What could we do to help them close the door on the year? And how might we help them start the next year well?'

These questions helped generate some excellent ideas on having a more structured approach to reviewing the year with the broader team and holding a formal kick-off session at the start of the next year.

The point here is that reviews can be a chance to more deeply connect with your team and increase emotional intelligence. That's not to say they have to be all warm-and-fuzzy. However, just as a pit stop can include lots of evidence-based conversations on strategy and productivity, it can also include some data on team relationships.

This can be delivered through a team survey – for example, using my Team Intelligence Diagnostic to track the team's EQ, IQ and PQ over time and then using the data to discuss trends and suggest tweaks to how the leadership team works.

Such a diagnostic allows the team to measure and discuss the key metrics that predict whether this team will become smarter than the sum of its parts.

In the diagnostic, you can then assess which elements (if any) of EQ are holding you back and refer to Part II of this book for ideas on how to unlock the team's emotional intelligence.

PIT STOP QUESTION 2: PQ AND PRODUCTIVITY

The Practical Intelligence (PQ) question is 'Are our delivery and project systems supporting the execution of strategy?'

When I'm working with leadership teams for the first time, I sometimes ask the group, 'How much of your time do you spend, in between leadership team meetings, on implementing the decisions and ideas from the meetings?'

One relatively new leadership team – within a start-up business unit in an ASX-100 company – gave their answers. On average it was about 5 per cent. As I mention earlier in this book, I asked the same group, 'How much do you want that to be?' They settled on 20 per cent, with the remaining 80 per cent spent on running their business units.

They were spending only a quarter of the time they wanted to on whole-of-business leadership issues – which meant, arguably, that they had formed more of a discussion group than a leadership team.

McKinsey's 'How to beat the transformation odds' suggests 24 questions to ask about your transformation efforts. One of them is, 'Do senior leaders and initiative leaders spend more than half their working time on the transformation?'

If the answer is yes, the odds of the transformation succeeding more than double (2.1 × increase, from 14 per cent to 30 per cent).

Now, that's not to say this time allocation is the right marker for you – after all, you may not be undergoing a radical transformation. Perhaps at times a leadership team can just lead their respective business unit and come together to share information. But these times seem increasingly rare. With the rate of change in business, most leadership teams are constantly battling change and transformation.

So, if you want to get good at turning your strategies, plans and ideas into real results, you need to have good practical intelligence and enough leadership time allocated to execute your plans.

My Team Intelligence Diagnostic also offers help here, allowing you to assess the practical intelligence of your team. How skilled are you at making robust plans, tracking progress and looking back to learn?

Along with this chapter, the previous two chapters have been all about giving you practical tips for each of those three leadership team skills. And having the ability to discuss these skills every quarter allows you to build the team's self-awareness and capability.

In a pit stop, if you are reviewing the team's practical intelligence or productivity, you may start to review specific projects. That can work, as long as you also spend time discerning the themes across projects. How good is the team at executing projects across the board? What is holding us back? What general systems might we need to change?

Given only 26 per cent of McKinsey's respondents said their transformation efforts had been successful (as discussed in chapter 8), it is incumbent on all leadership teams to close this gap between strategy and execution by reviewing and improving the team's practical intelligence.

PIT STOP QUESTION 3: IQ AND STRATEGY

Finally, the Creative-Analytical Intelligence (IQ) question for your pit stop is 'Can we strengthen our strategy?'

In 1928, Joseph Stalin set in motion the first of Russia's five-year plans, aimed at turning the country into an industrial powerhouse, and collectivising agriculture.

In 1961, John F Kennedy announced a plan to put a man on the moon within ten years. They did it in eight.

....
These days it is difficult to plan five or ten years ahead, especially if you aren't running a country.
....

As the external market evolves, you need to check in and see if your strategy still makes sense this quarter. Here are some questions you can ask:

- *Ambition questions:*
  - Is our ambition (or vision) still right?
  - Do the goals and projects we have in place get us there?
- *Analysis questions:*
  - When we wrote the strategy, did we use the right data?
  - Has any new data emerged?
  - Does the strategy still give us a winning position or competitive advantage?
- *Choices questions:*
  - Do the projects and strategic initiatives build on our strengths and values?
  - Are the choices we're making cohesive around a central narrative?
  - Have we honestly factored in risk and uncertainty?
  - What do we need to STOP doing?
- *Execution questions:*
  - Have we communicated the strategy to the broader team effectively?
  - Have we gathered feedback on progress from frontline staff?
  - Have we captured key learnings and adjusted plans accordingly?
  - What new obstacles are we facing, and do we have a plan to tackle them?

I call this a *strategy checklist*, and it can be used when you want to assess the strength of your leadership team's strategy. The following are two use cases in practice.

Leadership team 1

This functional leadership team in the financial services sector used the strategy checklist in a pit stop offsite, four months after creating an initial strategy. Based mainly on their learnings as a team from trying to explain and execute the strategy over the previous four months, they rated their strategy as average on a number of these questions. So, they took steps to strengthen it. The strategy gained a new lease of life and drove better results.

Instead of leaving an 'okay' strategy to slowly grow irrelevant, they made significant changes. This was based on a willingness to admit their previous work had become outdated.

Leadership team 2

An executive leadership team in the luxury goods sector conducted a series of workshops over four weeks to define a two-year strategy. Three weeks into strategy development, the team had a draft strategy done. Then they used the strategy checklist to surface some weaknesses. In this instance, the checklist allowed for robust discussion and was a pivotal checkpoint to surface constructive disagreement. Two main discussions emerged. First, was the strategy ambitious enough? Or was it 'more of the same'? And second, was the project roadmap realistic given current workload?

These insights allowed the team to learn from their work and make improvements.

Learning to improve

In both leadership teams, the ultimate outcome is for the team members to learn what makes a strategy better – or worse – and create a collective intelligence that they can use to improve today's strategy and next year's strategy.

The strategy checklist is specific to strategy development. But that is by no means the extent of a leadership team's creative-analytical challenges.

Therefore, a section in my Team Intelligence Diagnostic also asks the team to rate itself on going deeper, thinking wider and seeing further.

These two diagnostics can be used in conjunction. The Team Intelligence Diagnostic can be used every quarter to assess the leadership team's progress on the three types of intelligence.

And then the strategy checklist can be added in to have people rate one of the specific outputs of their collective intelligence: their long-term business strategy.

Chapter summary

Most leadership teams spend too little time learning from their successes and failures. Holding a half-day or full-day 'pit stop' four times per year represents an investment in deep learning and meaningful optimisation of the leadership team's collective intelligence.

Through considering critical questions about your relationships (EQ), strategy (IQ), and productivity (PQ), your leadership team can monitor its progress over time and improve its own understanding, capability and effectiveness.

Take action
Take advantage of reviews and pit stops in the following ways:

- Use short after-action reviews after significant moments and projects using the Intent>Actuality>Causation>Take-away framework.
- Diarise quarterly pit stops across the next 12 months and centre them on a small number of critical questions for the leadership team to consider.
- Include questions such as, 'Does our strategy need updating?', 'How can we get better at delivering projects?' and 'Do our relationships in the team need attention?'

- Give each pit stop a slightly different focus to maintain interest – for example, include a client deep dive, strategy planning, year-in-review, or personal leadership development on top of the three questions.
- Run my Team Intelligence Diagnostic before holding the pit stop.
- Recruit a facilitator to give structure to the pit stops.

Next

In the final part of this book, I run through the three journeys of leadership, and help you put together a complete 365-day roadmap for your leadership team's development. As you'll see, pit stops play a significant role. But they are not enough on their own.

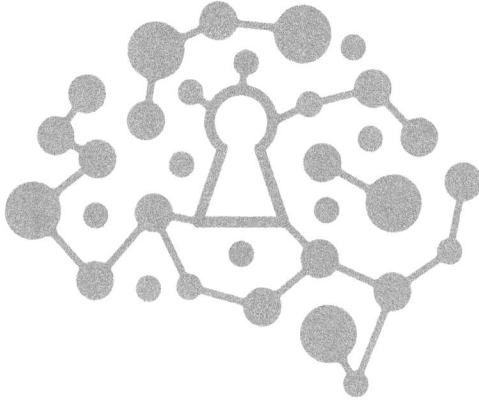

PART V

THE LEADERSHIP
TEAM'S JOURNEY

BUILDING A TEAM SMARTER THAN THE SUM OF ITS PARTS

'Maybe it's me?' said Frank.

He'd been building a leadership team for the last few months. Progress was good, but not perfect. His four divisional leaders had come together, developed a two-year strategy, launched it to the organisation, updated the structure and worked on the culture.

A specific focus for the whole organisation was to improve accountability. Stories abounded of unfinished projects and initiatives barely started before they were forgotten about.

Frank was pleased with initial progress. But there were bumps in the road. Some friction remained in the leadership team. And not all their projects were hitting targets. Frank decided that, as the leader, he needed to elevate his own leadership skills to lead the top team effectively.

Frank opted to review his leadership skills and asked for feedback from six of his staff.

The feedback (perhaps not surprisingly) centred on his accountability. Each of his direct reports gave Frank great feedback for his people skills, but they also said he could be better at holding people to account for delivering on their commitments.

This is not a rare finding in my experience. When we start talking about accountability, everyone is ready to name it as an issue. They are happy to suggest others should be more accountable. But few people point the finger at themselves.

Frank was one of the few. He admitted that he didn't like confrontation, so sometimes didn't step up to deal with issues.

However, Frank wasn't about to take all of the responsibility for this. Shouldn't senior executives be holding themselves to account without having to be reminded and nagged?

Once Frank and his leadership team were able to discuss the underlying issues around accountability, they could broker a solution that involved significant improvements in the leadership team's self-accountability and changes to Frank's consistency and timeliness on follow-up.

Frank was able to balance realistic demands on the leadership team with a level of openness and humility about his skills.

Of the many CEOs I've worked with, I'm pleased to report that the majority have a level of personal humility that helps them. In Australia, where I do most of my work, the stereotypical arrogant and solo CEO is relatively rare.

In the chapters in this part, I take you through the journey leaders need to go on, similar to Frank's, both with their team and individually. I pull together all the elements covered throughout this book, and outline the 365-day leadership team roadmap – laying out your journey ahead.

12

Learning.
The three journeys of the leadership team.

THE THREE JOURNEYS OF LEADERSHIP

As John Donahoe, former CEO of eBay and current CEO of Nike, noted, 'Leadership is a journey, not a destination. It is a marathon, not a sprint. It is a process, not an outcome.' If leadership is a journey, what kind of journey is it? And what does it mean for leadership teams?

The 'hero's journey' is an archetypal structure for storytelling. It underpins many movies, and has six steps: we meet the hero; we learn about the hero's everyday life; the hero faces a sudden challenge; the hero goes on a journey to find the solution, facing more challenges on the way; the hero discovers an answer; the story ends happily.

Leadership is not a hero's journey. The ending is rarely neat. Thinking of the leader as the hero is not useful. And their journey is not much like a movie.

Instead, leadership is three interconnected journeys:

1. *An inner journey:* A journey of learning for the leader or the leadership team.

2. *An outer journey:* The journey of achievement and moving towards a strategic goal, or a vision.
3. *A higher journey:* The journey towards meaning, your north star or purpose.

The way these three types of journey interconnect is shown in table 12.1.

Table 12.1: The three journeys of leadership

	Type	Periodicity	Benefits
Journey of learning	Inner journey	Quarterly	Insight
Journey of achievement	Outer journey	Annually	Completion
Journey of meaning	Higher journey	Career-long	Wisdom

The learning journey

The learning journey is made of deliberate experiments. Hindsight is not a great teacher, so learning is an active and ongoing process of setting intentions and assessing outcomes. This might include a quarterly cycle. And it results in generating useful insights that give you a deeper understanding of the complex adaptive system you work in.

....
No matter where you start relative to your competition, if you learn more quickly than they do, you will always win in the end.
....

The journey of achievement

The journey of achievement is the primary focus of the modern organisation. Being Number 1. Winning Awards. Hitting Goals. Ever since Neanderthals Inc went toe to toe with Homo Sapiens Pty Ltd 70,000 years ago, winning has been an essential part of the human psyche. Humans seem to be easily motivated by clear strategy, targets and competition.

The journey of meaning

The journey of meaning – to find your purpose or your north star – was popularised by Simon Sinek in *Start with Why*. Sinek proposed that organisations do better when their people share a deeper sense of 'why we exist'. Are we making a dent in the universe? Who are we here to serve? Sinek's work has proved more difficult in practice than in theory. Unless you have a good 'origin story' the idea of creating a purpose or developing a mission can seem hollow. And if it's the creation of the current CEO (or leadership team), then it only lasts as long as they do. Nonetheless, most leadership teams aspire to make a positive impact and leave a legacy. That can be a valuable journey to embark on, even if it has many risks and potential dead ends.

Aligning your journeys

The leader's job is to align these three journeys. The leadership team's learning journey should be aligned with the achievement journey: the deliberate experiments tie into the strategic roadmap.

And the achievement journey should be aligned with the meaning journey: the strategy should not just be based on where you are today and how you plan to get better and beat your competitors. It should also be based on a deeper sense of why the organisation exists.

In this chapter, I explore how to take a leadership team on these three journeys.

LEADERS NEED THREE TYPES OF INTELLIGENCE TOO

In 'The mindsets and practices of excellent CEOs', McKinsey gathered a range of empirical data on what makes CEOs effective. They considered six critical elements of the CEO's job:

1. setting the strategy
2. aligning the organisation
3. leading the top team
4. working with the board
5. being the face of the company externally
6. managing your own time and energy.

I argue that McKinsey's model and dozens of other leadership models can be explained more simply if we consider that leadership requires three types of intelligence:

1. emotional intelligence (EQ) to motivate people
2. practical intelligence (PQ) to drive productivity
3. creative-analytical intelligence (IQ) to set the direction and solve problems.

It is no coincidence that these are the same skills leadership teams need – leadership teams are just a collective approach to solving for organisational leadership.

However, the CEO's role does involve some specific elements that do not fall to the leadership team.

When coaching senior leaders one-on-one, I use the same three types of intelligence, but emphasise the different range of skills underpinning them, as shown in figure 12.1.

Notice that emotional intelligence has five layers underpinning it for individual leaders, starting with self-leadership and moving out to external relationships. In the middle of those five layers is team-building. This refers to the leader's work creating the environment for the leadership team's members to become a real team.

In addition, the work of 'leading a leadership team' involves managing yourself (for example, becoming a leader who speaks last) and managing individual relationships with the leadership team's members (EQ). It means leading strategy development and solving problems (IQ). And it requires a healthy dose of productivity, effectiveness and efficiency (PQ).

To build a team smarter than the sum of its parts, you need to start with a base level of each type of intelligence yourself. Then you must create the environment for your leadership team so they can improve on what you've got.

As a group, you should have robust emotional intelligence and healthy working relationships within a real team. You should drive collective action. And you should have a collective IQ that solves problems better than you as the leader could do on your own.

The result of an effective leadership team is intelligent collective action.

As the leader of the top team, the requirement of you is to unlock the team's hidden intelligence to get there.

THE TEAM JOURNEY

In 2020, leaders and their leadership teams were faced with a stream of challenges related to COVID-19. Depending on your industry, demand dropped or surged. Overnight, your whole organisation learnt to work at home. Your leadership adapted to daily crisis meetings while learning to team remotely.

In June 2020, I surveyed 40 leadership team members as part of Leading Out of Lockdown, a live online event. How did their leadership teams react to these crises?

....

During COVID-19, 63 per cent of leaders reported: 'my leadership team has performed more effectively than it normally does'.

....

Leaders reported the experiences during COVID-19 forced them to be more creative and make decisions more quickly. They had to make a lot more decisions, including more solo decisions, as well

Figure 12.1: The individual leadership framework

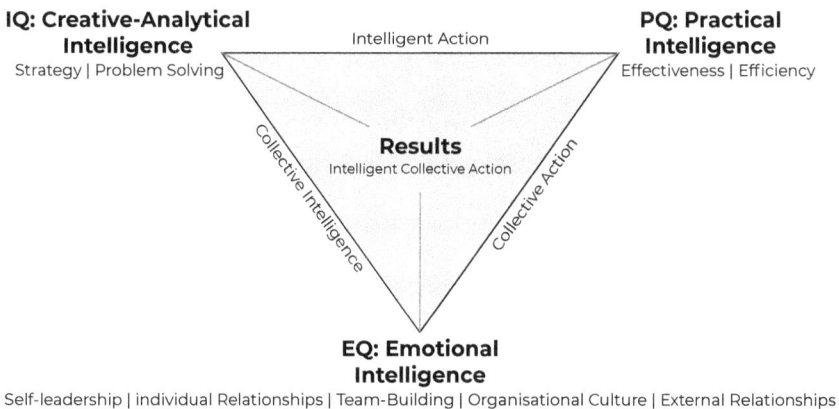

IQ: Creative-Analytical Intelligence
Strategy | Problem Solving

Intelligent Action

PQ: Practical Intelligence
Effectiveness | Efficiency

Collective Intelligence

Results
Intelligent Collective Action

Collective Action

EQ: Emotional Intelligence
Self-leadership | individual Relationships | Team-Building | Organisational Culture | External Relationships

as more decisions involving other people. They had to get better at communicating decisions to the broader team.

Qualitatively, leaders reported a sense of focus (we have one common enemy: the virus); being able to prioritise the critical issues; coming together to solve problems quickly; and having less time for internal politics.

In November 2020, I ran an event called Hindsight 2020 and asked another pool of leaders, 'How much can you learn about leadership from 2020 compared to a normal year – less, the same or more?'

Every single leader chose 'more'.

Teams learn more when the pressure is on.

Instead of assuming you can only build effective leadership teams in the classroom or on an offsite, you can also look to four types of experience to develop your TEAM:

- *Trials:* Challenges that require the team to collaborate under moderate pressure – a key tender, a competitive threat, or even a pandemic. These are trials for the leadership team to undergo and learn from.
- *Experiments:* Innovative projects or test-and-learns provide ways to learn and improve. These should be deliberate experiments, with clear intentions at the outset. Without clear intentions, you can only learn from hindsight, which is not a reliable teacher.
- *Achievements:* Celebrating and rewarding achievements helps build a team, of course. This works better when the team's incentives are based on team performance. Successful projects can also be worth post-analysing to understand why they worked.
- *Mistakes:* This involves admitting mistakes and learning from them with regular post-analysis, which should then be used to make immediate changes to upcoming projects.

The leader of the team can look for these opportunities to learn and build the team. Trials and experiments can be identified in advance and managed as prospective opportunities to come together, innovate and learn. Achievements and mistakes are retrospective opportunities to learn by conducting regular reviews.

....

Don't wait for an annual offsite. The best opportunity for the leadership to learn and grow is through taking a learning mindset to its real day-to-day work.

....

COMBINING TEAM EXPERIENCES WITH PLANNED INTERVENTIONS

In 'High-performing teams: A timeless leadership topic' from McKinsey, authors Scott Keller and Mary Meaney note: -

> Most [leadership teams] will benefit from a program that purposefully mixes offsite workshops with on-the-job practice. Offsite workshops typically take place over two or more days. They build the team first by doing real work together and making important business decisions, then taking the time to reflect on team dynamics.

Learning-from-real-work is an effective – indeed essential – strategy for any leadership team. However, it's not enough to unlock the full intelligence of the team. When you are racing to meet deadlines and complete projects, the opportunity for learning can be limited. That's because team learning requires intention, collaboration, experimentation and reflection (see, for example, *Teaming* by Amy Edmondson).

Leadership teams need to set a collective intention for how they want to work. This includes laying the foundations for emotional intelligence and behavioural norms. I call this the *set up*.

Leadership teams need to regularly assess whether they are on track. I call this the *check-in*.

Leadership teams also need to take time off the racetrack to reflect and consider what they've learnt and how they optimise their activities when they get back on the track. I call these *pit stops*.

And, finally, leadership teams need to use their collective intelligence to define a direction – a strategy and plan. This is the *strategy workshop*.

In the next chapter, I explore the details of each of these planned interventions.

Chapter summary

The leader's role is to take the leadership team on a journey. In fact, three journeys: a learning journey, a journey of achievement and a journey towards a meaningful purpose.

To do this, and build a leadership team that becomes more than the sum of its parts, you'll need to use three types of intelligence as the leader. Your emotional intelligence to build a real team. Your creative-analytical intelligence to lead strategy development. And your practical intelligence to make a plan for your leadership team and ensure real progress.

The plan, or roadmap, for your leadership team journey can take in a range of ad hoc experiences – including trials, experiments, achievements, mistakes.

Take action

Take your leadership team on the journey with the following:

- Gather 360 feedback from your team to help you refine your leadership style and understand your strengths in the three types of intelligence.
- Use the real work of the team to learn together, to celebrate achievements and to connect to the team's purpose, or meaning.
- Trials, experiments, achievements and mistakes (TEAM experiences) are your biggest opportunities for discussion and learning for the leadership team.

Next

In the next chapter, I take you through a year in the life of your leadership team, outlining my 365-day leadership team roadmap.

13

Leveraging.
Shaping the growth of the leadership team.

'I feel like this is my 20th lap around the same track.'

Chris is a senior executive who has worked in the same industry for many years. I met him one January for lunch at a sunny café on the beach in Sydney. Despite the temperate weather, he was struggling to get himself into gear for his 20th year in his industry. It felt like 'just another lap around the track', with the same kinds of conversations, and the same kinds of problems.

Chris's comment illustrates the following aspects of the leadership journey:

- First, the journey has a natural cadence. Depending on where you are in the world, there may be a natural break in the year. In Australia, many organisations close for around three weeks over December–January. In Europe, some companies largely shut down in July. These breaks offer natural opportunities for the CEO to shape the journey. Also, many companies have a quarterly rhythm, which provides a natural opportunity to engage the team in reflection and planning. What did we learn from the last quarter? How do we optimise the next quarter?

- Second, if you don't give the leadership team a direction, they can feel like they're on a hamster wheel, running fast and going nowhere.

In Australia, I often recommend to leadership teams to end December with a reflection meeting to review the year and celebrate achievements; and then start the new year with a set-up (or 'kick-off') meeting to quickly ramp up the energy for the journey. These two sessions can effectively bookend the summer shutdown period.

THE 365-DAY LEADERSHIP TEAM ROADMAP

Let's zoom out and build on this thinking to consider a year in the life of a leadership team. The kinds of activities you and your leadership team could plan are included in the roadmap shown in figure 13.1. (Go to robpyne.online/unlock to download a copy of this framework.)

Figure 13.1: The 365-day leadership team roadmap

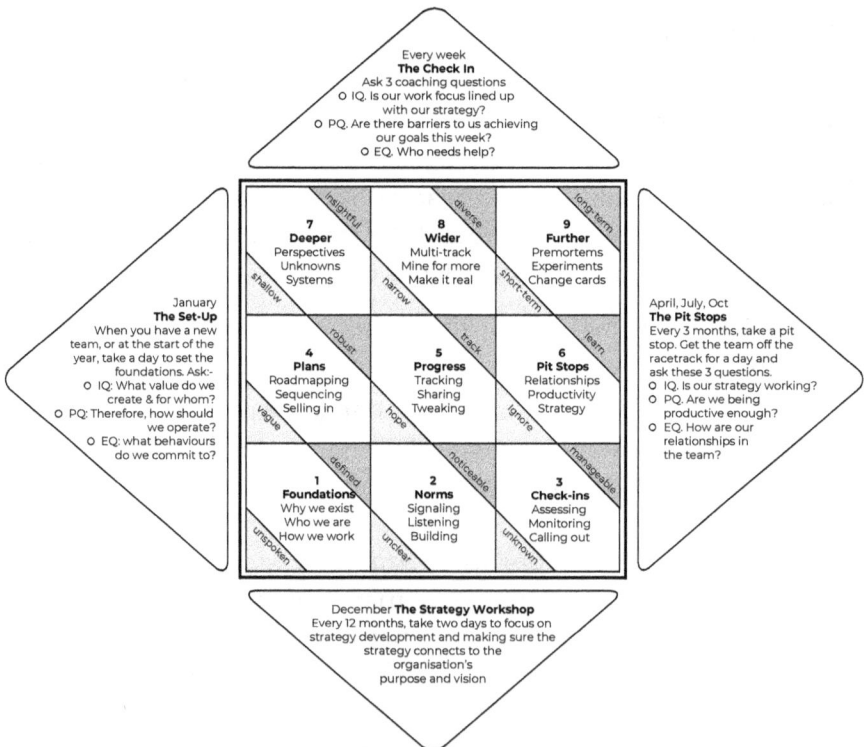

Every week
The Check In
Ask 3 coaching questions
O IQ. Is our work focus lined up with our strategy?
O PQ. Are there barriers to us achieving our goals this week?
O EQ. Who needs help?

7 Deeper — Perspectives, Unknowns, Systems (insightful / shallow)

8 Wider — Multi-track, Mine for more, Make it real (diverse / narrow)

9 Further — Premortems, Experiments, Change cards (long term / short term)

January
The Set-Up
When you have a new team, or at the start of the year, take a day to set the foundations. Ask:-
O IQ: What value do we create & for whom?
O PQ: Therefore, how should we operate?
O EQ: what behaviours do we commit to?

4 Plans — Roadmapping, Sequencing, Selling in (robust / vague)

5 Progress — Tracking, Sharing, Tweaking (track / hope)

6 Pit Stops — Relationships, Productivity, Strategy (team / ignore)

April, July, Oct
The Pit Stops
Every 3 months, take a pit stop. Get the team off the racetrack for a day and ask these 3 questions.
O IQ. Is our strategy working?
O PQ. Are we being productive enough?
O EQ. How are our relationships in the team?

1 Foundations — Why we exist, Who we are, How we work (defined / unspoken)

2 Norms — Signaling, Listening, Building (noticeable / unclear)

3 Check-ins — Assessing, Monitoring, Calling out (manageable / unknown)

December **The Strategy Workshop**
Every 12 months, take two days to focus on strategy development and making sure the strategy connects to the organisation's purpose and vision

The roadmap shown in figure 13.1 is centred on my nine building blocks of the leadership team. To unlock your leadership team's intelligence over a year, the four surrounding interventions can build your emotional intelligence (EQ), creative-analytical intelligence (IQ) and practical intelligence (PQ).

EQ, IQ and PQ can also be tracked quarterly using my Team Intelligence Diagnostic. (This diagnostic tool and a copy of the 365-day leadership team roadmap are available at robpyne.online/unlock.)

The roadmap is built for a company that works on a calendar-year focus, with quarterly rhythm. The intervention timings can be adjusted according to your organisation's rhythm – for example, if you have a financial-year focus.

The calendar builds on the excellent work from Richard Hackman, Ruth Wageman and Colin Fisher in 'Leading teams when the time is right: Finding the best moments to act' in which they advise leaders not to make team interventions in the middle of busy periods of work. They recommend finding natural opportunities at the beginning, middle or the end of major projects to take time out and reflect on team performance.

The following sections outline these points of reflection in my 365-day leadership team roadmap in more detail.

January: The set-up

The kind of set-up workshop your leadership team runs in January depends on whether you are a new or an existing team.

New leadership teams: Setting up the team

The focus for the set-up meeting here is on a new leadership team that needs to set the ground rules. This set-up meeting would typically be a full-day session, and can happen at any time of the year, of course – as soon as the leadership team is formed.

The agenda for this team set-up meeting would aim to answer the purpose, people and processes aspects – or the why, who and how – of the leadership team (refer to chapter 1). This meeting would also aim to create a platform to build the three types of team intelligence.

In particular, these aspects would then be used to build the emotional foundations of the leadership team (refer to chapter 3 for a full explanation of the importance of these foundations).

Your leadership team would ask itself:

- What value does this leadership team exist to create? And who are its stakeholders?
- Therefore, what different types of meetings should we have, and what should we talk about in each?
- How should we behave as a group – what behavioural norms do we commit to?
- How will we run and track leadership team projects?
- What resources and support do the team need to succeed?

The first four questions are covered at length in chapters 3, 4, 5, 9 and 10.

The fifth question around resources is inspired by the research of Ruth Wageman, Debra Nunes, James Burruss and Richard Hackman in *Senior Leadership Teams: What it Takes to Make Them Great*. The authors found the following resources differentiated effective leadership teams:

- *Rewards:* Leadership teams benefit when their incentives are team-based. And yet many retain incentives solely for their functional jobs. For example, suppose the chief revenue officer is only rewarded for revenue figures. In that case, she is more likely to act defensively around other topics that affect her team but do not drive revenue.
- *Education:* The team members often need to deepen their understanding of the whole business. In one strategy development project, we added a whole-day induction for the team members such as HR, Legal and Operations heads to understand the organisation's product mix and commercial strategy better.
- *Information:* Many leadership teams say they lack reliable, real-time business performance data. This data is essential for decision-making, and not having it has a measurable negative impact on leadership team performance. The leader needs to address any lack in reliable data.

- *Support:* Leadership team members need to have support in administration, personal assistance, time and materials. The leadership team's expectations should include a realistic percentage of their time allocated to advancing the leadership team's agenda as part of their day job. Suppose you, as the leader, expect their ongoing contribution to whole-of-business projects. In that case, it is not okay to treat these projects like 'hobbies' to be completed in their spare time after dedicating 110 per cent (or more) of their full-time hours to running their business unit.

Existing leadership teams: Setting up the year

For existing teams, the setting up the year workshop happens at the start of your year (financial or calendar) to set the team up for the year ahead. The workshop can last from two hours to a full day.

In Australia, where I live, many business-to-business organisations shut down just before 25 December, and then people trickle back to work any time in January. The leadership team risks losing a whole month of momentum. Instead, you want to gather the team at the starting line and quickly prepare everyone to get back up to full speed.

At this particular time of year, I advise leadership teams to consider four RAMP questions of their team and their wider team:

- *Reflection:* Have we closed off last year, celebrated achievements and adopted vital learnings?
- *Alignment:* Are we aligned on the strategy and goals for the year ahead?
- *Motivation:* How are our motivation levels? Have we ensured that individuals can see 'what's in it for them' this year?
- *Purpose:* Let's make sure everyone is connected to why this all matters; how does the year contribute to our purpose?

These four questions can define the agenda for a leadership team setting up the year workshop. They also prompt questions about a broader session for the whole organisation (or for business units) – how quickly can you get the entire team together to set up the year?

An example agenda for the leadership team's setting up the year workshop, building on the RAMP principles, could be as follows:

- *Reflection:* What were the high points, turning points and low points of last year? How did this team operate and what needs to change? What were the key insights, and how are we applying them this year? (This agenda item is required only if you didn't do a wrap-up meeting at the end of the previous year.)
- *Strategy alignment:* Do we need to refresh or update our strategy, or revisit the specific goals and project roadmap for the leadership team?
- *Team motivation:* Check in on the team's togetherness and emotional capital. How is each individual feeling about the year ahead? How can the team work better together? What team and personal development opportunities would be beneficial? Any other resources needed to succeed?
- *Reconnect to purpose:* Why does the coming year matter to our organisation's purpose? What's significant?

Think back to the story of Chris on his 20th lap. This workshop structure would help the Chrises in your team ramp up for the year.

Outputs of the set-up workshops

If you're setting up a new leadership team, the output of this workshop may include three tangible agreements. If you're setting up the year, you can introduce these or update them. The three agreements are:

- *The leadership team blueprint:* The defining agreements on why you exist, who you are, and how you operate can be captured in a blueprint document. This contains a page for each of the RAMP questions outlined in the previous section. The blueprint represents the recorded outcomes of the workshop and creates a lasting reminder of what was agreed. As the leader or member of the leadership team, you can then refer back to this during team meetings, and it can be used to revisit how the team is performing against its agreements.

- *The leadership team roadmap:* Setting the year's expectations, the leadership team can have a roadmap of the year indicating key leadership team meetings (pit stops, strategy workshops) and timings of deliverables. For example, one leadership team had predictable requests every year from US headquarters and decided to put them on the leadership team's roadmap. For more on roadmaps, refer to chapter 9.
- *The leadership team dashboard:* The dashboard measures the leadership team's development. It can be integrated into an overall development measuring the delivery of financials, strategy, projects. The team metrics would typically come from a tool such as my Team Intelligence Diagnostic and can be measured by quarterly surveys of the team itself, and six-monthly feedback from the team's stakeholders. For more on dashboards, refer to chapter 10.

Every week: The check-in

How often does your leadership team meet?

If the answer is monthly, you may be meeting too infrequently to deal with operational issues, support each other and build a real team.

....
Monthly meetings are for committees, not teams.
....

At the same time, monthly meetings may be too frequent to review the strategy and critical projects meaningfully.

That's why I recommend differentiating your meetings into a regular operational meeting and a less frequent series of pit stops.

Regular can mean:

- *Every day:* During the pandemic in 2020, one leadership team I work with met at 9 am every day. After a while, this moved to three times a week.
- *Every week:* Another team I work with meets for 90 minutes each week to address operational issues and assign actions.
- *Every fortnight:* A third team meets for two hours every fortnight.

The exact frequency needs to suit your organisation's operational speed and your leadership team's value agenda. If you've agreed your leadership team is solely strategic, weekly meetings won't be necessary.

Three team coaching questions for your check-in

These check-in meetings, around weekly in frequency, will always struggle to get through an agenda everyone is happy with.

They will no doubt be operational in focus and deal with many reactive issues. Those could include trials, experiments, achievements and mistakes (for more on the TEAM journey, refer to chapter 12).

As the leader or member of the leadership team, you do have the chance to turn these TEAM experiences into learning opportunities through team coaching.

Team coaching

One of the most consequential actions you can take is to coach the team. In *Senior Leadership Teams: What it Takes to Make Them Great*, the authors' research found:

> Outstanding teams had significantly more coaching, both from leaders and from one another, than did mediocre and struggling teams. The most significant influence on peer coaching – how much team members coached one another – was how much the team leader coached them. When you coach your team, the members gradually begin to intervene in their own processes in increasingly constructive ways.

The authors did not find that one-to-one coaching of individual members improved the team's performance. It was coaching of the whole team. How does this work specifically?

Team coaching is designed to keep the team on track and to help it focus on how it creates value. It can keep the team focused on the right high-value issues, and can minimise the time spent on tangents.

Team coaching starts with the leader. You'll need to adopt a coach's approach, considering the content and dynamics of the meeting. To do this, you need to temporarily separate yourself from the content and become a 'fly on the wall' for a few seconds. Ask yourself, 'Is this meeting on track?' If it is, get back into the content. If not, adopt a coach's mindset and consider what question you can ask the team to get back on track.

If you can role-model this coaching behaviour, other leadership team members can step up and ask these helpful questions too, over time. You'll have created an environment where the team is self-aware and able to self-regulate.

The three questions
Coaching can be defined as the process of helping people solve their own problems by asking questions. When it comes to coaching teams, the questions you could ask in an operationally focused check-in meeting are:

- *The IQ question:* Is our work focus lined up with our strategy?
- *The PQ question:* Do barriers exist to us achieving our goals this week?
- *The EQ question:* Who needs help?

These questions connect the operational flow of a check-in meeting to the three types of team intelligence. They should be helpful to the operational flow. They should not derail the discussion.

When not to coach
This coaching approach is more likely to add value if you have already built the team's emotional capital and behavioural norms. If this is not the case, some team members will find it useful, and others may question it and consider it counterproductive.

Besides, coaching is a process of questioning and inquiry, acting to help the team solve its own problems. That's different from the CEO shutting down a discussion unilaterally with a comment such as, 'We're off track, let's get back to the discussion on forecasting.' If you steer the meetings too actively, over time, the team can feel disempowered.

The exception to this is when you need to call out a specific behaviour, where you may want to pause the meeting and have a one-to-one chat with the person in question. Refer to chapter 5 for more on calling out unhelpful behaviour.

April, July and September: Pit stops

We covered pit stops in detail in chapter 11. The idea of a pit stop is to 'get off the racetrack' for a day for renewal and to refuel.

Renewal is the word McKinsey use in their article 'High-performing teams: A timeless leadership topic'. Their research suggests one of the characteristics of effective top teams is that:

> [They] take time to renew – evolving, innovating, learning from the broader context, and investing in individual and team-wide development.

It is helpful to schedule these pit stops or renewal points just before, or at, the start of each quarter. Typically, they are a full day (which equates to around six hours of working time after breaks are accounted for).

The idea of renewal – and the related concept of wellbeing – is an increasingly strong focus for leadership teams.

In a recent year-in-review meeting with a successful team, each team member committed to a plan of 'self-care' for their own wellbeing. The CEO explicitly endorsed the importance of wellbeing in his team and committed to quarterly pit stops for them to take time for renewal.

As the team plans quarterly opportunities to 'refuel', you will want to combine a structured program of pit stops over the year with flexibility on the agenda. This flexibility allows for reacting to how the team is feeling at the end of each quarter, and what specific challenges they face.

Part of the pit stop should be dedicated to live projects and real work (focusing on only the highest value, strategically important work).

And the rest of the pit stop can be used to reflect and renew and address the three types of intelligence your team needs.

The three questions

The three questions you may want to ask at each pit stop are:

- *The IQ question:* Is our strategy working?
- *The PQ question:* Are we being productive enough?
- *The EQ question:* How are our relationships in the team?

Here's a typical schedule for a quarterly pit stop that uses the three questions and allocates time to tackling a real work issue:

1. *Strategy review:* Using the AACE – ambition, analysis, choices, execution – strategy checklist tool to rate the strategy and identify areas to strengthen. (To download the checklist, go to robpyne.online/unlock.)
2. *Productivity review:* Looking at the visible project roadmap, and the team's dashboard, how are we tracking? What have we learnt, what can we change as a result?
3. *Team review:* How much emotional capital have we built? Are any behaviours holding us back from being more successful collectively?
4. *Specific strategic issue:* Going deep into one strategic issue that needs to be understood, solved or actioned.

Each of the first three areas can be supported by my pre–pit stop Team Intelligence Diagnostic (see robpyne.online/unlock.). The diagnostic can also suggest new behaviours to use when discussing the live strategic issues.

For example, if the diagnostic reveals the team is weak on conversational turn-taking, they can tackle the strategic issue with a strong emphasis on hearing from each team member.

Other inclusions in pit stops

If you have pit stops in April, July and September, assigning a different focus for each can be helpful. For example:

- April's pit stop could focus on customers. Go on a customer tour in the morning (for example, observe customers buying your product, or go to a customer office). Or bring a customer in to be interviewed (I have seen these work well to change the conversation's focus from internal to external). If your organisation claims to be 'customer-centric' you may still find large parts of the leadership team are disconnected from customers and never leave the building.

- July's pit stop could include a focus on self-development. To facilitate this, you could include external speakers, education on the wider business, understanding competitors and getting to grips with the financials.
- September's pit stop could focus on innovation. You could bring in speakers who highlight future trends, customer insights and competitive innovations.

In practice, having these focuses highlighted at the start of the year makes the pit stops more motivating for the leadership team.

Having one of the pit stops at a distant location (Fiji, Bali, Hunter Valley or Byron Bay, perhaps?) creates a sense of reward and helps create a real team. 'Time in the bar', where team members have time to build shared team stories, does have benefits too.

Pitfalls for pit stops

Here are additional do's and don'ts for running pit stops, offsites and away days.

First, the do's:

- Do plan the schedule in detail, working back from the key questions you want to answer.
- Do plan the schedule and length of the event based on having six workable hours a day (9 am to 5 pm minus break times is six hours).
- Do include real work, not just team building.
- Do bring in external voices only if they add specific value – and only for a short time.
- Do ask the team to do pre-work – for example, preparing data or analysis ready for discussion, or considering solutions to a problem.
- Do brief everyone on what's expected of them – for example, specific roles or pre-work may be required from individuals.
- Do make use of my Team Intelligence Diagnostic to elevate the conversation around the team's performance.

- Do communicate the reason for the offsite and the desired outcomes to your broader organisation.
- Do include some team-building activities (but no more than 20 per cent of the time).
- Do allocate 10 per cent of the time to finalise actions and make specific follow up plans.
- Do book a venue with plenty of space and natural light.
- Do use an external facilitator, so the CEO doesn't have to plan the meeting and act as a facilitator.

And now the don'ts:

- Don't take the team to Fiji for a week if you're cutting jobs (sounds obvious, but I've seen it done).
- Don't drink at lunchtime.

December: The strategy workshop

Can you fit your business strategy on one page?

One of the most successful leadership teams I've worked with introduced me to this practice. The reasons I recommend it are:

- Strategy is about hard choices, and having to simplify your strategy to fit on one page encourages hard choices – as long as the discussion before each choice is rich.
- The strategy needs to be communicated to the broader team to affect their behaviour. The one-page format is excellent for this.
- Each team member needs to see how they fit into the strategy. And how the strategy fits together. The visualisation of a house allows for both.

....

You get to simplicity by going through complexity and coming out the other side

....

I call the model I use to facilitate strategy development for leadership teams the strategy house, as shown in figure 13.2 (on the following page).

Figure 13.2: The strategy house

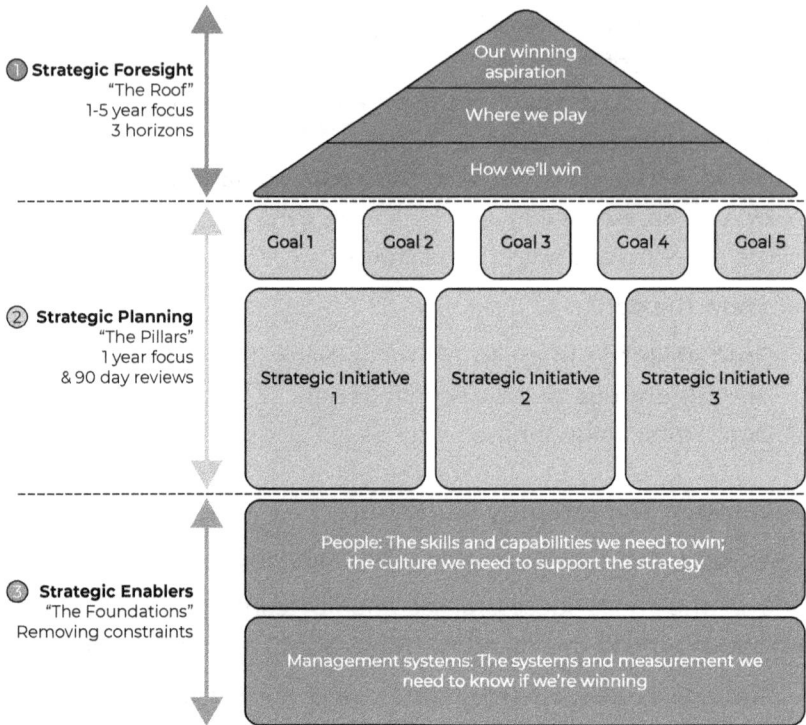

① Strategic Foresight
"The Roof"
1-5 year focus
3 horizons

- Our winning aspiration
- Where we play
- How we'll win

② Strategic Planning
"The Pillars"
1 year focus
& 90 day reviews

Goal 1 · Goal 2 · Goal 3 · Goal 4 · Goal 5

Strategic Initiative 1 · Strategic Initiative 2 · Strategic Initiative 3

③ Strategic Enablers
"The Foundations"
Removing constraints

People: The skills and capabilities we need to win; the culture we need to support the strategy

Management systems: The systems and measurement we need to know if we're winning

Working with your leadership team to create the organisational strategy house is the culmination of all your work to unlock the team's intelligence.

You have created the emotional foundations where everyone feels safe to contribute their unique knowledge and highlight gaps, and ask great questions.

You have built the creative-analytical intelligence for the team to go deep into understanding the real issues and root causes of problems. As a team, you also go wide to consider multiple solutions, not just the first one you think of. Your team is able to put the Kool-Aid on ice and make realistic predictions of success.

You have harnessed the team's practical intelligence to turn the strategy into a roadmap showing how the key initiatives may play out over time, along with a dashboard to measure them.

More on strategy

The strategy house I've developed builds on a few of the many strategic frameworks you can find, including those outlined in:

- *Playing to Win: How strategy Really Works* by Alan G. Lafley and Roger Martin
- *Blue Ocean Strategy* by Renée Mauborgne and W. Chan Kim.

For a copy of the Strategy House, head to robpyne.online/unlock.

In this section, I am not covering how to write a business strategy; I am focusing on how to unlock the team's intelligence to use any strategic framework well.

Here are the do's and don'ts of strategy workshops. The do's:

- Do get feedback and ideas from the frontline – listen to your frontline managers and ask for their contribution.
- Do name any decision-makers who aren't in the room. If it needs board approval, build in time for it.
- Do have the right number of people. Ideally, you have five to eight people developing the strategy. If your leadership team is more than eight people, that's okay, just build in more time to develop the strategy.
- Do agree on a strategic framework, and a process, and explain it to the leadership team upfront.
- Do allow enough time for the team to work through complex issues. A one-day strategy workshop can get you started but will not get the whole strategy finished, let alone include the development of all the roll-out plans. Either schedule a multi-day offsite or book a series of half or one-day workshops over several weeks.
- Do convert the strategy into a visible project roadmap to show the sequence of activities that need to happen.
- Do develop a dashboard that measures the strategy, as well as financial (and other) outcomes.
- Do convert the thinking into a communication plan, and cascading goals for the wider team.
- Do update the strategy regularly, making tweaks to strengthen it.

- Do make sure you have trustworthy data, such as customer insights and trends analysis, to inform your choices.

And now the don'ts:

- Don't try to create the strategy in half a day.
- Don't assume anyone will remember the strategy unless you explain it well and talk about it every week.
- Don't treat the strategy as 'finished' – it's just a work in progress and can be strengthened over time by regularly reviewing it in the quarterly pit stops.
- Don't overcommit or undercommit. The strategy is a bet; you're making a bet that if you do A and B, then you'll get result X and Y. Most business plans and strategies don't work as initially envisioned, so be open to changing course when good new evidence is presented. Don't change your mind otherwise – keep committed.

Chapter summary

Your leadership team's year should include a series of planned interventions, including set-up workshops, check-ins, pit stops and strategy workshops.

As you may have noticed, these interventions reflect the metaphor of a Formula One team – setting up the car, tracking progress, refuelling, and then taking time to plan the development of next year's car.

This chapter pulls together the nine building blocks of your high-performing, fast-moving team and creates a 365-day roadmap to be competitive in your industry race.

Take action
Here's how to get started on your leadership team's 365-day roadmap:

- If you have a new leadership team or one that needs a complete reset, start with a team set up workshop, and at the end of that, agree on the roadmap for the rest of the year, covering check-ins, pit stops and strategy workshops.

- If you have an existing leadership team, start with running my Team Intelligence Diagnostic, and then run a setting up the rest of the year workshop. In this, you can agree on the roadmap for the rest of the year, covering check-ins, pit stops and strategy workshops.
- If you're about to develop a strategy with your leadership team, you'll want to focus on the strategy workshop. However, before you get stuck into strategy, you may want to run the Team Intelligence Diagnostic and establish new behavioural norms to use while creating the strategy. At the end of strategy development, take time to reflect on what you learnt about yourself as a team.

Next

In the conclusion, I explore a metaphor that helps make sense of all the ideas in this book.

Conclusion

THE RUBIK'S CUBE OF LEADERSHIP TEAMS

At age 35, I had an operation that kept me out of the surf for six weeks. Surfing was (and remains) my main hobby, so I decided to use the extra time to create a list of 40 things to do before 40. In those few short weeks, I even managed to tick one of them off: I learnt to solve the Rubik's Cube in less than two minutes.

Solving a Rubik's Cube on your own is hard. But if you learn from someone who has done it before, read their book and follow their instructions carefully, you can learn it.

Leadership teams are also complicated, with lots of moving parts.

Like the Rubik's Cube, I have suggested several building blocks that need to be solved to get a leadership team working.

While we have talked a lot about the moving parts in this book, only one person is the solver.

You.

You hold in your hands the infinite possibilities of leadership.

You can choose to try your own moves and solutions.

And you can also choose to build on the experience and real-world solutions of others.

The solutions I present in this book are by no means mine alone. I am deeply indebted to the authors, facilitators and leaders I've encountered these last years.

I hope I have taken their solutions and added my own shortcuts and tweaks to make it easier for leaders to learn and apply the appropriate techniques and solve their leadership team puzzles.

BUILDING A SOLUTION, LAYER BY LAYER

Leadership, more than ever before, is a collective role. Leadership teams are essential to provide the organisation the right direction, a strong culture and the tools and resources to make progress.

The problem leaders face, their Rubik's Cube, is how they unlock the hidden intelligence in their leadership teams. This 'unlocking' is how you bring a group of people together and build a team that is smarter than the sum of its parts.

The hidden intelligence has three layers, just like the approach to solving a Rubik's Cube:

- You first solve the bottom layer: the team's emotional intelligence.
- Then you solve the middle layer: the team's creative-analytical intelligence.
- And finally, you solve the top layer: the team's practical intelligence.

Leading the top team – solving these layers – is one of the most valuable things a CEO can do. As the authors stress in McKinsey's 'High-performing teams: A timeless leadership topic', senior leaders operating in a high-performing leadership team are five times more effective. Your challenge is to create the environment to unlock this potential.

NEXT STEPS

Each of the chapters is designed to be self-contained. Even if you've read the book cover to cover, you can still dip back into chapters as needed. For example, if you find you want to work on how your team comes together to understand issues before they rush to develop a solution, head to chapter 6. Read it and then look at the action plan at the end of the chapter.

In addition, chapters 12 and 13 bring the whole book together as a 365-day roadmap for you to lead your leadership team on a journey. Chapter 13 makes recommendations for planning your year if you need to form a leadership team, if you need to fix an existing leadership team, or if you need to work with your leadership team to develop a strategy or solve a significant problem.

Many leaders choose to get additional support when they develop their leadership team. A book can take you so far, but it does not plan the offsite, collect data on your team, or facilitate a year's worth of growth in your team.

If you choose additional support, extra resources and services are available at robpyne.online/unlock to help you turn what you've read into real results with your leadership team.

A FINAL WORD

Leadership teams can feel like the best of times, and they can feel like the worst of times. Although this book focuses on effectiveness, I hope that being in a leadership team inspires you, stretches you and makes you feel like I did when playing Dungeons and Dragons in 1984.

May your leadership team meetings be the highlight of your month.

References and further reading

Listed below are the books and articles I've referenced through this book, along with others that were most useful to me in researching the existing schools of thought on leadership teams.

Allan, D, Kingdon, M, Murrin, K and Rudkin, D (2002), *Sticky Wisdom: How to Start a Creative Revolution at Work*, 2nd edition, John Wiley & Sons UK)

Boroş, S and Vîrgă, D (2020), 'Too much love will kill you: the development and function of group emotional awareness', *Team Performance Management*, 26. (1/2): 71–90.

Bourke, J (2017), *Which Two Heads Are Better Than One? How Diverse Teams Create Breakthrough Ideas and Make Smarter Decisions*, Australian Institute of Company Directors.

Buehler, R, Messervey, D and Griffin, DW (2005), 'Collaborative planning and prediction: Does group discussion affect optimistic biases in time estimation?' *Organizational Behavior and Human Decision Processes*, 97(1):47–63.

Carse, JP (2013), *Finite and Infinite Games: A Vision of Life as Play and Possibility*, Simon & Schuster USA.

Clear, J (2018), *Atomic Habits: An Easy and Proven Way to Build Good Habits and Break Bad Ones*, Random House UK.

Cross, R, Rebele, R and Grant, A (2016), 'Collaborative overload', *Harvard Business Review,* Jan-Feb 2016: 74-79.

de Bono, E (2017), *Six Thinking Hats*, Penguin UK.

Dewar, C, Hirt, M and Keller, S (2019), 'The mindsets and practices of excellent CEOs', McKinsey.

Duke, A (2018), *Thinking In Bets: Making Smarter Decisions When You Don't Have All the Facts*, Penguin Group USA.

Edmondson, A (2012), *Teaming: How Organizations Learn, Innovate, and Compete in the Knowledge Economy*, Jossey-Bass USA.

Edmondson, A (2018), *The Fearless Organization: Creating Psychological Safety in the Workplace for Learning, Innovation, and Growth*, John Wiley & Sons Inc USA.

Gemünden, HG, Hauschildt, J (1985), 'Number of alternatives and efficiency in different types of top-management decisions', *European Journal of Operational Research*, 22, (2): 178–190.

Gigerenzer, G (2015), *Risk Savvy: How to Make Good Decisions*, Penguin UK.

Green, DW, Over, DE and Pyne, RA (1997), 'Probability and choice in the selection task', *Thinking & Reasoning*, 3(3), 209–235.

Grenny, J, Patterson, K, Maxfield, D, McMillan,R and Switzler, A (2013), *Influencer: The New Science of Leading Change*, McGraw-Hill Education USA.

Hackman, RJ, Wageman, R and Fisher, CM (2009), 'Leading teams when the time is right: Finding the best moments to act', *Organizational Dynamics*, 38(3): 192–203.

Haidt, J (2007), *The Happiness Hypothesis: Putting Ancient Wisdom to the Test of Modern Science*, Random House UK.

Heath, C and Heath, D (2011), *Switch: How to Change Things When Change is Hard*, Random House UK.

Heath, C and Heath, D (2013), *Decisive: How to Make Better Choices in Life and Work*, Random House UK.

Herb, E, Leslie, K and Price, C (2001), 'Teamwork at the Top', *McKinsey Quarterly*, Spring 2001: 39.

Isaacson, W (2015), *The Innovators: How a Group of Hackers, Geniuses, and Geeks Created the Digital Revolution*, Simon & Schuster UK.

Jacquemont, D, Maor, D and Reich, A (2015), 'How to beat the transformation odds', McKinsey Quarterly April 2015.

Kahneman, D (2012),*Thinking, Fast and Slow*, Penguin UK.

Kaner, S, and Lind, L (2014), *Facilitators Guide to Participatory Decision-Making*, Jossey-Bass USA.

Kaufman, J (2010), *The Personal MBA: Master the Art of Business*, Penguin UK.

Keller, S, and Meaney, M (2017), 'High-performing teams: A timeless leadership topic', *McKinsey Quarterly*, June 2017: 81-87.

Klein, G (2007), 'Performing a project premortem', *Harvard Business Review*, Sept 2007: 1-2.

Klein, G (2017), *Sources of Power: How People Make Decisions*, Random House USA.

Komisar, R (2010), 'How we do it: Three executives reflect on strategic decision making', *McKinsey Quarterly*, March 2010: 46-57.

Kotter, J (2012), *The Heart of Change: Real-Life Stories of How People Change Their Organizations*, Harvard Business Review Press USA.

Lafley, AG, and Martin, R (2013), *Playing to Win: How Strategy Really Works*, Harvard Business Review Press USA.

Lencioni, P (2012), *The Five Dysfunctions of a Team*, 2nd edition, John Wiley & Sons Inc USA.

Liveris, C, quoted in Liddy, M and Hanrahan, C (2017), 'Fewer women run top Australian companies than men named John — or Peter, or David', ABC News, 8 March 2017.

Lovallo, D and Sibony, O (2010), 'The case for behavioural strategy', *McKinsey Quarterly*, March 2010.

Mauborgne, R and Chan Kim, W (2015), *Blue Ocean Strategy: How to Create Uncontested Market Space and Make the Competition Irrelevant*, Harvard Business Review Press USA.

Mitchell, DJ, Russo, JE and Pennington, N (1989), 'Back to the future: Temporal perspective in the explanation of events'. *J. Behav. Decis. Making*, 2: 25–38.

Mullins, J and Komisar, R (2009), *Getting to Plan B: Breaking Through to a Better Business Model*, Harvard Business Review Press USA.

Neatby, J (2016), 'The ballooning executive team', *Harvard Business Review*, July 2016.

Pink, D (2018), *Drive: The Surprising Truth About What Motivates Us*, A&U Canongate.

Quirke, Bill (2007), *Making the Connections: Using Internal Communication to Turn Strategy Into Action*, Gower Publishing UK.

Rego, A, Owens, B, Leal, S, Melo, A, Pina e Cunha, M, Goncalves and Ribeiro, P (2017), 'How leader humility helps teams to be humbler, psychologically stronger, and more effective: A moderated mediation model', *The Leadership Quarterly*, 28: 639-658.

Reynolds, A and Lewis, D (2017), 'Teams solve problems faster when they're more cognitively diverse', *Harvard Business Review*, March 2017.

Ries, E (2011), *The Lean Startup: How Constant Innovation Creates Radically Successful Businesses*, Penguin UK.

Schulz, K (2011), *Being Wrong: Adventures in the Margin of Error*, Granta UK.

Senge, P (2006), *The Fifth Discipline: The Art and Practise of the Learning Organisation*, Doubleday & Co. USA.

Sinek, S (2011), *Start with Why: How Great Leaders Inspire Everyone to Take Action*, Penguin UK.

Sinek, S (2020), *The Infinite Game*, Penguin UK.

Sniezek, J and Henry, R (1989), 'Accuracy and confidence in group judgment', *Organizational Behavior and Human Decision Processes*, 43: (1): 1-28

Souman, JL, Frissen, I, Sreenivasa, MN and Ernst, MO (2009), 'Walking straight into circles, *Current Biology*, 19 (18): 1538–1542.

Sunstein, C and Hastie, R (2015), *Wiser: Getting Beyond Groupthink to Make Groups Smarter*, Harvard Business Review Press, USA.

Tamm, J (2015). 'Cultivating collaboration: Don't be so defensive!' TEDx Talk, 26 May 2015.

Tetlock, PE and Gardner, D (2016), *Superforecasting: The Art and Science of Prediction*, Crown Publishing Group USA.

Tuckman, B (1965), 'Developmental sequence in small groups', *Psychological Bulletin*, 63 (6): 384–399.

Wageman, R, Nunes, D, Burruss, J and Hackman, R (2008), *Senior Leadership Teams: What it Takes to Make Them Great*, Harvard Business Review Press USA.

Wiseman, L (2010), *Multipliers: How the Best Leaders Make Everyone Smarter*, HarperCollins USA.

Woolley, AW, Chabris, CF, Pentland, A, Hashmi, N and Malone, TW (2010), 'Evidence for a collective intelligence factor in the performance of human groups', *Science*, 330(6004): 686–688.

Zak, P (2017), *Trust Factor: The Science of Creating High-Performance Companies*, HarperCollins Focus USA.

Appendix: The key ideas in this book

I've provided here a list of the ideas and tips I have found most useful when working with leadership teams, broken down by the chapters in this book.

Chapter	EQ – Emotional intelligence ideas
3	*Identify your value agenda* Ask: what value does the team create, and for whom? Then prioritise so you can see the value agenda
3	*The boundaries of the team* Ask: who's in this team and why? And how can you be a real team, not just a meeting or a committee?
3	*Operational rhythm* Ask: how do you create value, what do you talk about, how do you meet, how do you make plans and track progress?
4	*Signal your respect* Set behavioural norms that help team members feel liked, respected and competent. Make sure you signal your recognition.
4	*Make them feel heard* Use active listening skills to make people feel heard – including body language, paraphrasing and building.

4	*Dialogue beats debate* Build on and add to others' comments; use collective thinking. Avoid competitive thinking where the best idea wins.
5	*Check in with the team* At the start of your meetings, take time to check in how people are – in their work life and their home life.
5	*Take the temperature* Monitor the emotions in the room; make sure people don't get personal. Ask for people's gut reaction to ideas.
5	*Call out bad behaviour* If you see destructive behaviours, pause the meeting and have a one-to-one coaching chat with that person. Take time to reflect on meetings.
Chapter	**IQ – Creative-analytical intelligence ideas**
6	*Take a perspective tour* Look at a situation from other perspectives: outcomes, options, process, people, evidence, risk.
6	*Explore the unknowns* Be clear on what you do and don't know. Ask: what's the big picture? What does success look like? What do you know from the past?
6	*Understand the system* Use systems thinking to understand how one moving part affects another and how one action can have many consequences.
7	*Generate three options* When you have a problem, generate three potential solutions, and one recommendation.
7	*Use diamond-shaped thinking* Spend the first half of a meeting in 'divergent thinking' generating lots of ideas. Then move to convergent thinking and drive to a decision.

7	Compare options side by side
	Shortlist your two best options, flesh them out and compare them side by side on your criteria for success.
8	Conduct a premortem
	Before you press 'go' on an idea, imagine it's 12 months in the future and the idea failed. Why did it fail?
8	Run experiments
	Before you go 'all-in' on a decision, can you run an experiment to test your plan, and measure the results?
8	The 24 change cards
	Use the 24 Change Checklist Cards to check your change management plan is robust and realistic.
Chapter	**PQ – Practical intelligence ideas**
9	Visible project roadmap
	Make a roadmap of the year with three to four lanes (business areas) and add all the critical projects onto the map.
9	Strategic sequencing
	For each quarter, add the single most important project to the roadmap, and then add any other projects that can work well in conjunction with it.
9	Communicating your plan with the three Es
	Communicate your strategy and roadmap to the wider team with empathy, explanation and expectation.
10	Make a progress dashboard
	Create a dashboard that tracks performance, projects, pacing and patterns.
10	Communicating progress is two-way
	Regularly ask your team for updates on how they are going delivering the strategy, and share back the overall results.
10	Changing course: will you bet, check or fold
	Use external data and internal data to decide whether to keep going (bet), pause (check) or pull the plug (fold).

11	*Measure your team dynamics* Use the Team Intelligence Diagnostic to assess the EQ, IQ and PQ of your team every three months and track progress.
11	*Measure your productivity* Every three months, assess project delivery metrics and look for any patterns that are holding you back from delivering your commitments.
11	*Strengthen your strategy* Use the strategy checklist (rating your ambition, analysis, choices, execution) to assess your strategy every three months and make changes to it.

About the author

Rob studied psychology at University College London, specialising in human judgement and decision-making. In 1997, he quit his PhD to move to Australia and surf. He joined the world of advertising, rising to become Chief Strategy Officer of global agency Initiative. After a series of leadership roles, Rob set up training firm Realizer in 2013, with a mission to help the world make better decisions. He discovered that the best way to improve decision-making is to work with leadership teams – to unlock their collective intelligence. This book is based on the latest research into leadership teams – and Rob's insights from working with more than 50 teams and hundreds of leaders.

For more help

Every year I take on new clients to help them unlock the intelligence in their leadership team.

I can be reached through my website robpyne.online or on email at rob@robpyne.online if you would like to discuss partnering over a year, running a one-off workshop, or speaking opportunities.

ONLINE RESOURCES

Head to robpyne.online/unlock for the following:

- the Team Intelligence Diagnostic
- the joystick questioning model (chapter 6)
- the 24 Change Checklist Cards (chapter 8)
- the AACE strategy checklist (chapter 11)
- an example of an individual leadership framework (chapter 12)
- the 365-day leadership team roadmap (chapter 13)
- an example of the strategy house (chapter 13)
- example agendas for check-ins, pit stops and kick offs (chapter 13)